US Citizenship Test Study Guide 2026 and 2027:

Updated Naturalization Exam Prep with all 128 USCIS Civics Questions and Answers

[5th Edition]

B. Hettinger

Copyright ©2025 by Trivium Test Prep

ISBN-13: 9781637988121

ALL RIGHTS RESERVED. By purchase of this book, you have been licensed one copy for personal use only. No part of this work may be reproduced, redistributed, or used in any form or by any means without prior written permission of the publisher and copyright owner. Trivium Test Prep; Accepted, Inc.; Cirrus Test Prep; and Ascencia Test Prep are all imprints of Trivium Test Prep, LLC.

The Department of Homeland Security, US Citizenship and Immigration Services, was not involved in the creation or production of this product, is not in any way affiliated with Trivium Test Prep, and does not sponsor or endorse this product.

Image(s) used under license from Shutterstock.com and Library of Congress

Table of Contents

Introduction vii

About the Test vii
About This Guide vii

Part 1 United States Government 1

1 The US Constitution 3

Historical Context of the US Constitution 3
Basics of the US Constitution 5
Types of Powers 8
Amending the Constitution 10
Civil Liberties and Rights 12
Answer Key 15

2 The Legislative Branch 17

The Legislative Branch 17
The House of Representatives 19
The Senate 21
Lawmaking 23
Answer Key 26

3 The Executive and Judicial Branches 27

The Executive Branch 27
Electing the President 31
The Judicial Branch 33
Answer Key 38

4 American Political Systems 39

Political Parties 39
Interest Groups and Mass Media 42
Answer Key 45

Part 2 United States History 47

5 Early North America 49

North America Before European Contact 49
England and the Thirteen Colonies 55
Conflict in the Thirteen Colonies 58
Answer Key 62

6 Revolution and the Early United States 63

The American Revolution 63
Federalists and Democratic-Republicans 66
Foundations of Westward Expansion 69
Early United States 72
Answer Key 75

7 Civil War, Expansion, and Industrialization 77

Roots of the US Civil War 77
Aftermath and Reconstruction 80
The Gilded Age 84
Answer Key 88

8 The United States Becomes a Global Power — 89

Socioeconomic Change and World War I 89
The Great Depression in the United States . 91
The United States and World War II 94
Answer Key 97

9 Postwar and Contemporary United States — 99

Cold War, Liberalism, and Social Change 99
The Civil Rights Movement 101
The Rise of Conservatism 104
The End of the Cold War 106
Answer Key 109

10 Geography and Civics Facts — 111

United States Geography 111
The United States Today 114
Civics Facts 119
Answer Key 123

11 USCIS Civics Test — 125

Answer Key 129

Introduction

About the Test

Congratulations on becoming a United States citizen! By purchasing this book, you've taken an important step on your path to citizenship. This book will help prepare you for the oral civics examination you will take as part of your US citizenship process.

What's on the Test?

The Civics Test is administered by the United States Citizenship and Immigration Services (USCIS), part of the Department of Homeland Security. The Civics Test consists of 20 questions. It is NOT multiple choice, but most practice tests made available, including those from the US government, are multiple choice. There is a bank of 128 questions used for the test. USCIS makes the 128 questions available at **https://www.uscis.gov/sites/default/files/document/questions-and-answers/2025-Civics-Test-128-Questions-and-Answers.pdf**.

A USCIS officer will ask you these questions in person. Your officer will choose 20 questions from the bank of 128. The test is administered in English, and you must answer the questions in English.

Scoring

To pass the test, you must answer 12 of the 20 questions correctly.

The 65/20 Consideration

If you are above the age of 65 and have legally lived in the United States for at least 20 years, then you're eligible for special consideration. In this case, you should ONLY study the questions which are marked with an asterisk (*). The USCIS officiant will ask you 10 questions from the pool of 20 questions that are marked an asterisk. You must answer 6 of those 10 questions correctly in order to pass.

About This Guide

This guide will help you master the most important test topics and develop critical test-taking skills. Along with a detailed summary of the test's format, content, and scoring, we offer an in-depth overview of the content knowledge required to pass the test. Throughout the guide, you'll find sidebars that provide interesting information, highlight key concepts, and review content so that you can solidify your understanding. You can also test your knowledge with sample questions throughout the text as well as practice questions. We're pleased you've chosen Trivium to be a part of your journey!

PART 1
United States Government

1 The US Constitution

Historical Context of the US Constitution

Any study of the United States government must begin with its founding document: the Constitution. It was written as both an expression of ideals and as a practical framework for the functioning of the country. Designed to be a "living document," the Constitution and how it is interpreted has changed in the almost 230 years since it was written. However, its core principles have not. They continue to serve as the foundation and guiding light of American government and politics.

While it is tempting to view the Constitution as a timeless document, it is important to understand that it was actually very much a product of the time in which it was written. The ideals that inform it grew directly out of the Enlightenment, and the governing structure it created was in direct response to both colonial discontent under Britain and problems faced by the new republic. In order to understand the government that emerged, it is necessary to understand this context.

While influenced by philosophy, the Constitution is actually a very practical document. It lays out the overarching structure of the government without excessive detail, explanation, or justification. However, each decision made about the structure of the government was an attempt to either prevent the re-emergence of tyranny or fix the mistakes of the first, failed government.

 HELPFUL HINT
Written in 1787, the Constitution is the supreme law of the land.

Articles of Confederation

In 1781, when it was all but assured that the colonies would win the Revolution, the Second Continental Congress had convened to organize a government for the emerging nation. The colonies had broken away from Britain, in short, because of what they viewed as the oppressive rule of an over-bearing central government. As a result, the first government they created, whose framework was called the Articles of Confederation, was intentionally weak. Called a "firm league of friendship," it was designed to create a loose confederation between the colonies (now states) while allowing them to retain much of their individual sovereignty.

As a result, the Articles established a political system which consisted of a **unicameral legislature** (only one house) with extremely limited authority. The Congress of the Confederation, as it was called, did not have the power to levy taxes or raise an army. Any laws had to be passed by a two-thirds vote, and any changes to the Articles had to be passed unanimously—essentially an impossible feat. The legislature was intentionally and clearly subordinate to the states. Representatives were selected and paid by state legislatures.

It quickly became clear that this government was too weak to be effective, and by 1787, the new government of the United States, only six years old, was already in crisis. Without the power to levy taxes, the federal government had no way to alleviate its debt burden from the war. In addition, without an organizing authority, states began issuing their own currencies and crafting their own competing trade agreements with foreign nations, halting trade and sending inflation through the roof. Without a national judicial system, there was no mechanism to solve the inevitable economic disputes.

Shays' Rebellion

Discontent was particularly strong among farmers, who were losing their property at devastating rates. Their unhappiness exploded into violence in 1786 when Daniel Shays led a rebellion against Massachusetts tax collectors and banks. Unable to raise an army, the Congress of the Confederation was powerless to intervene. The rebellion was finally suppressed when citizens of Boston contributed funds to raise a state militia. **Shays' Rebellion** made it clear that the new government was unable to maintain order.

Rule of Law

The founders of the United States were all very learned men who were educated in the philosophy of the Enlightenment. Several key elements of this philosophy are reflected in the Constitution.

HELPFUL HINT

Rule of law means everyone must follow the law.

The very desire for a written constitution—a law above all others—reflected Enlightenment thinking, as it ensures a **rule of law**, rather than a rule of man. In a nation ruled by man, governance is at the whim of an individual or small group of individuals. Decisions are arbitrary based on the interests and needs of those in authority. In a nation ruled by law, governance is based on a body of written, or otherwise codified, law (such as the Constitution). No individual can make a governing decision in conflict with those laws.

Reason

The Constitution is a document based on **reason** and is therefore relatively simple and straightforward. It lays out the structure of government without detailing every single function of that government. Rather than simply empowering authority, the Constitution aims to limit government while still allowing it to fulfill its function. It also insists that governing decisions are made outside the scope of religion, by actively separating the two.

Social Contract

The document begins "We the People…" because the founders believed that government was a **social contract**, legitimized only by the consent of the people. This is also known as **popular sovereignty**—the concept that people should govern themselves. The Constitution protects individual liberty, life, and property, the fundamental natural laws laid out by John Locke.

Social Progress

Enlightenment thinkers believed strongly that **social progress** was possible. As a result, the writers of the Constitution built in a means for amending the Constitution, allowing it to progress with the nation it governed.

Influences

A number of other historical documents had an influence of the writing of the Constitution, including the Declaration of Independence, Articles of Confederation, Mayflower Compact, Iroquois Great Law of Peace, Federalist Papers, Antifederalist Papers, Fundamental Orders of Connecticut, and the Virginia Declaration of Rights.

REVIEW QUESTIONS

1. What is the Constitution based on?

2. What philosophical movement informed the ideals of the US Constitution?

3. Under the Articles of Confederation, the legislature was subordinate to whom?

4. What did Shays' Rebellion prove about the early US government?

5. Why did the writers of the Constitution build in a way to amend the document?

Basics of the US Constitution

Constitutional Convention

A convention of the states was called to address problems in the young United States. At the **Constitutional Convention** in 1787, a decision was made to completely throw out the old Articles and write a new governing document from scratch. There were five main goals for the new Constitution:

1. the protection of property
2. granting increased, but limited, power to the federal government
3. the protection of and limitations on majority rule
4. the protection of individual rights
5. the creation of a flexible framework for government

Each of these reflect the desire to balance authority and liberty. It is this balance that is at the core of the framework of the American government.

Checks and Balances

The crises of the 1780s made it clear that a stronger central government was needed. However, the states did not want a central government that was so strong that it would oppress the states or the people. The solution? Increase the power of the government but prevent the concentration of power by dividing it.

The federal government was reorganized under the Constitution, shifting from a one-body political system to a three-branch system as conceived by Montesquieu. In addition to a now bicameral (two house) legislature, a legitimate executive branch was added as well as a judicial. Following Montesquieu's model of **separation of powers**, the now-increased powers of the federal government were divided between these branches. In addition, each branch was given powers that would limit the power of the other branches in a system called **checks and balances**. For example:

- The executive branch—via the role of president—has the power to veto (reject) laws passed by the legislature.
- The legislative branch can override the president's veto (with a two-thirds vote) and pass the law anyway.
- The judicial branch can determine the constitutionality of laws (**judicial review**).

The president has the power to appoint justices to the federal courts (including the Supreme Court), and the legislative branch—via the Senate—has the power to approve or reject presidential appointments.

The legislative branch also has the power to indict, try, and determine the guilt of a president. The indictment may only be for treason, bribery, and other "high crimes and misdemeanors." While not specifically defined in the Constitution, this is traditionally taken to mean crimes that are specific to office holders.

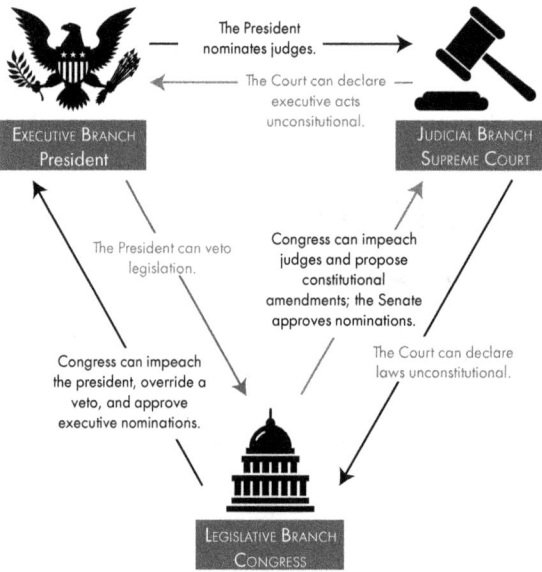

Figure 1.1. Checks and Balances

These include perjury, abuse of power, misuse of funds, and dereliction of duty.

Almost immediately upon the ratification of the Constitution, it began to grow and now includes a massive bureaucracy made up of departments and agencies.

Federalism

The separation of powers limited the powers within the federal government, but did not address the power relationship between the federal government and the states. Under the Articles, the federal government was completely beholden to the states for its very existence. However, it was clear that complete state sovereignty did not work. Instead, the Constitution created a **federal** relationship between the two levels of government. **Federalism** is a system in which both the state government and federal government retain sovereignty by dividing up the areas for which they are responsible.

Under the Constitution, the federal government is charged with matters that concern the population at large: for example, handling federal lands, coining money, and maintaining an army and navy. It also handles conflicts between the states via the federal judiciary and by regulating interstate trade. Matters of regional or local concern are handled by state or local governments.

This relationship is best codified in the Tenth Amendment, which states that any powers not explicitly given to the federal government are reserved for the states or the people. However, according to the **supremacy clause** (Article 6, Clause 2) the Constitution is the "supreme law of the land." Therefore, in cases of conflict between the states and the federal government, the federal government's authority generally supersedes that of the states. The division of power has shifted over time with more power going to the federal government as its scope has expanded.

The federal government also can exert influence over state governments through **grant-in-aid**, money that is provided for a particular purpose. The federal government can attach stipulations to this funding. For example, grant-in-aid was given to the states in the late 1970s for highway improvement. However, states who accepted the money were required to set the drinking age at twenty-one years old in their state. This was a way for the government to influence law that was technically beyond their purview.

REVIEW QUESTIONS

6. The authors of the US Constitution sought to balance which TWO seemingly competing principles?

7. The term "checks and balances" means what?

8. What is the process by which the judicial branch determines the constitutionality of laws?

9. What TWO governments divide up responsibilities under federalism?

10. How can the federal government exert influence over state laws?

Types of Powers

Governmental powers in the Constitution can be divided into six types:

Expressed Powers

Also known as **enumerated powers**, expressed powers are powers that are specifically granted to the federal government only. An example of an expressed power is the power to make treaties with foreign nations.

Reserved Powers

Reserved powers are powers that are held by the states through the Tenth Amendment, which states that all powers not expressly given to the federal government belong to the states. For example, the management of public education is a reserved power.

Concurrent Powers

Concurrent powers are powers that are shared equally by both the national and state government. The power to tax and the power to establish courts are both concurrent powers.

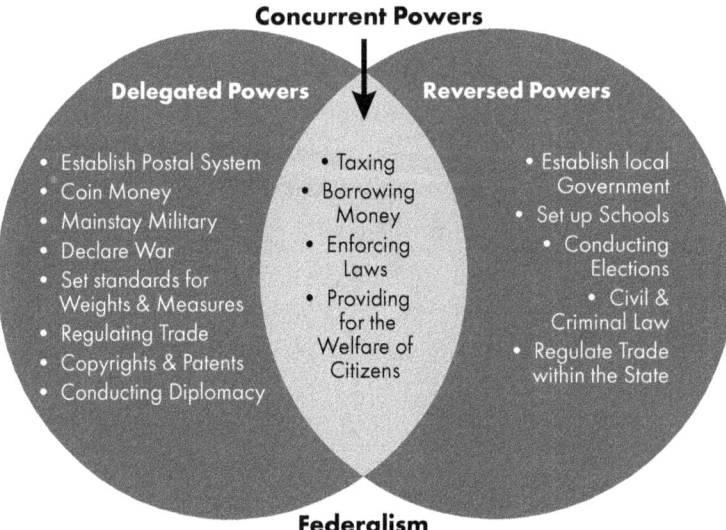

Figure 1.2. Enumerated, Concurrent, and Reserved Powers

Implied Powers

Implied powers are powers the federal government has that are not in the Constitution. They derive from the elastic clause of the Constitution, Article I, Section 8. The **elastic clause** gives Congress the right to "make all laws necessary and proper" for carrying out other powers. For example, over time as new technologies have emerged, such as radio and television, the commerce clause has been expanded to allow the federal government to regulate them.

The idea of implied powers was supported by the Supreme Court in *McCulloch v. Maryland* (1819). The state of Maryland tried to tax the Maryland branch of the Bank of the United States. When the bank refused to pay the tax, the case landed in the Maryland Court of Appeals; the court ruled that the Bank of the United States was unconstitutional, as the Constitution did not expressly give the federal government the power to operate a bank. Later, the Supreme Court overturned the ruling, citing the elastic clause.

DID YOU KNOW?

The elastic clause, Article I, Section 8, Clause 18 of the Constitution, authorizes Congress "To make all laws necessary and proper to the execution of the other expressed powers."

Inherent Powers

Inherent powers are powers that derive specifically from US sovereignty and are inherent to its existence as a nation. For example, the powers to make treaties and to wage war are both inherent powers.

Prohibited Powers

Prohibited powers are powers that are denied to both the national government and the state governments. Passing bills of attainder (laws that declare someone guilty without a trial) is a prohibited power.

REVIEW QUESTIONS

11. Which powers are granted to the federal government only?

12. What does the elastic clause grant Congress?

13. Implied powers refer to powers that are not listed in which document?

14. Which powers are held by the states through the Tenth Amendment?

15. What are examples of concurrent powers?

THE US CONSTITUTION

Amending the Constitution

HELPFUL HINT

Two-thirds is a magic number in American government. Two-thirds of Congress is needed to 1) override a veto, 2) propose an amendment to the Constitution, or 3) remove a president, judge, or other civil official after impeachment (Senate only).

Congress is responsible for another significant legislative process: amending the Constitution. The framers understood that they could not possibly foresee every threat to state sovereignty and personal liberty nor every need that would require government management. So they added Article V to the Constitution, which lays out a procedure for amending it. This is one of the most significant aspects of the Constitution as it makes it a "living document."

Amendments to the Constitution can either come from Congress or from the state legislatures. For Congress to propose an amendment to the Constitution, two-thirds of each house must vote in favor of the amendment.

Alternatively, an amendment can be proposed if two-thirds of the states call for a national constitutional convention. All amendments to date, however, have been proposed by Congress. Either way, once the amendment has been officially proposed, it is not ratified until three-quarters of state legislatures (or special conventions convened by each state) approve it.

The Bill of Rights

HELPFUL HINT

There are twenty-seven amendments to the Constitution, the first ten of which were passed immediately in 1791.

These first ten amendments, now called the **Bill of Rights**, were a condition for ratification imposed by people who thought the new government wielded too much power. These **anti-federalists** argued that individual liberty had to be explicitly protected from federal intervention. Thus, the Bill of Rights protects the rights of Americans and people in the United States. According to the amendments, the government may not:

- Amendment I: prohibit freedom of religion, speech, press, petition and assembly
- Amendment II: prohibit the right to bear arms
- Amendment III: quarter troops in citizens' homes
- Amendment IV: conduct unlawful search and seizures
- Amendment V: force anyone to testify against themselves or be tried for the same crime twice
- Amendment VI: prohibit the right to a fair and speedy trial
- Amendment VII: prohibit the right to a jury trial in civil cases (the original Constitution only guaranteed a jury in criminal cases)
- Amendment VIII: force citizens to undergo cruel and unusual punishment
- Amendment IX: violate rights that exist but are not explicitly mentioned in the Constitution
- Amendment X: usurp any powers from the states not given to them in the Constitution (so all other powers not listed in the Constitution belong to the states)

Unofficial Changes to the Constitution

While the only official way to change the Constitution is through the amendment process, other loopholes for change exist within its framework. These include:

Clarifying Legislation: Using the **elastic clause**, much legislation has been passed whose purpose is to clarify or expand the powers of the federal government. For example, the Constitution only provides directly for the Supreme Court, but empowers Congress to create other courts. The Judiciary Act of 1789 created the federal judiciary.

- **Executive Actions**: Although Congress holds most lawmaking power, the president is able to issue executive actions which have the force of law without having to involve Congress. The most famous of these is Abraham Lincoln's Emancipation Proclamation.

- **Judicial Decisions**: In *Marbury v. Madison* (1803) the Supreme Court established the precedent of **judicial review**, the power of the Supreme Court to determine the constitutionality of laws. *Marbury v. Madison* not only illustrated how judicial decisions can expand federal power in general, but it also broadened the power of the Supreme Court in particular, laying the groundwork for future decisions that would have a similar impact.

- **Political Parties**: The rise of political parties changed the political landscape as well. Some aspects of American politics—like how the Speaker of the House is chosen and nomination conventions for presidential candidates—have come from political parties rather than through a formal legislative process.

Prohibited Powers

Although Congress was made much more powerful by the Constitution, a real fear of tyranny existed among the framers. While Section 8 of the Constitution lists the powers of Congress, Section 9 lists what Congress cannot do. Most notable are:

No suspension of habeas corpus: A writ of habeas corpus is a legal demand a prisoner can make to appear in court in order to profess their innocence. Basically a means of preventing unreasonable imprisonment, this was viewed as an essential element of a just government. The Constitution forbids its suspension except in cases of rebellion or invasion. (Note: Abraham Lincoln, during the Civil War, was the first president to suspend habeas corpus.)

No bills of attainder: A bill of attainder is a law that declares an individual or a group guilty of a crime without holding a trial. Much like with the writ of habeas corpus, this was seen as an essential protection in a fair society.

No ex post facto laws: An ex post facto law is a law which punishes an individual or group for breaking a law that was not a law when the act was committed. For example, slavery was abolished in 1865. If an ex post facto law was passed at that time, it would have punished anyone who had owned slaves before 1865.

No titles of nobility: It was important to the framers to provide safeguards against a return to monarchy. Therefore, they prohibited an American nobility of any kind.

REVIEW QUESTIONS

16. Which groups can propose amendments to the Constitution?

17. Why did anti-federalists want the Bill of Rights?

18. How many amendments does the US Constitution have?

19. What does an executive action allow the president to bypass?

20. What does section 9 of the Constitution list?

Civil Liberties and Rights

Influenced by the ideas of the Enlightenment and fresh from revolution, the framers of the Constitution valued **civil liberties**. Civil liberties are rights—provided for either directly by the Constitution or through its historical interpretations—which protect individuals from arbitrary acts of the government. The framers protected some liberties explicitly in the Constitution via the prohibited powers and expanded on them in the Bill of Rights. Each of these amendments restricts the actions of the federal government rather than actually granting a freedom to the people.

The First Amendment

Speech: The liberties most central to the American identity are articulated in the First Amendment: speech, press, petition, assembly, and religion. The first four are all closely related. No liberty is truly unlimited, however, and the court has imposed restrictions on speech over time. It has upheld laws banning libel, slander, obscenity, and symbolic speech that intends to incite illegal actions.

Religion: The freedom of religion comes from two clauses in the First Amendment: the **establishment clause** and the **free exercise clause**. The first prohibits the government from establishing a state religion or favoring one religion over another. The second prohibits the government from restricting religious belief or practice. Again, this is not unlimited. The court has found that religious practice can be banned if it requires engagement in otherwise illegal activity. There are also continuing debates on allowing prayer in schools and granting vouchers to students to attend parochial schools.

Rights of the Accused

Most of the civil liberties written into the body of the Constitution addressed the rights of the accused, including prohibitions on bills of attainder, ex post facto laws, and denials of writs of habeas corpus. Three of the amendments in the Bill of Rights address this as well.

The **Fourth Amendment** restricts unlawful searches and seizures. In *Mapp v. Ohio* (1961), the Supreme Court ruled that evidence obtained illegally—so in violation of the Fourth Amendment—could not be used in court. This **exclusionary rule** is very controversial, and the courts have struggled since to determine when and how to apply it.

The **Fifth Amendment** protects the accused from self-incrimination. Drawing on this amendment, the Supreme Court ruled in *Miranda v. Arizona* (1966) that arrestees must be informed of their due process rights before interrogation in order to protect them from self-incrimination. These rights, along with those in the Sixth Amendment, are now colloquially known as **Miranda rights**.

The **Sixth Amendment** guarantees the accused the right to a fair, speedy, and public trial, as well as the right to counsel in criminal cases. While originally this only applied at the federal level, in *Gideon v. Wainwright* (1963) the Supreme Court ruled that states must provide counsel to those who cannot afford it.

The Fourteenth Amendment

The Court's ruling in *Gideon v. Wainwright* was based on the Fourteenth Amendment's **equal protection clause**. Ratified in 1868, the amendment's original purpose was to ensure the equal treatment of African Americans under the law after the abolition of slavery. However, its use has been expanded far beyond that original purpose.

The equal protection clause has been used to protect the **civil rights**—protections against discriminatory treatment by the government—of individuals of a variety of groups. Equality is a tricky concept for Americans. It is central to the American ideology, a guiding principle of the Declaration of Independence: "All men are created equal…"

The courts have regularly protected political and legal equality, as well as equality of opportunity (like the *Brown v. Board of Education* decision in 1954). However, the courts do not recognize a right to economic equality. The Supreme Court also recognizes the need for reasonable classifications of people, and allows discrimination along those lines. For example, age restrictions on alcohol consumption, driving, and voting are all considered constitutional.

The Supreme Court has also used the Fourteenth Amendment over time to extend federal civil liberties to the state level. Today, all states are held to the same standard as the federal government in terms of civil liberties.

HELPFUL HINT

Use the acronym RAPPS to remember the freedoms of the First Amendment: (R)eligion, (A)ssembly, (P)etition, (P)ress, and (S)peech.

Due Process: The second part of the Fourteenth Amendment extends the Fifth Amendment's due process guarantees to the state level. "No person shall be deprived of life, liberty or property without the due process of law..." While this typically refers to the processes of the accused, as discussed above, it has also come to represent certain unnamed, or implied, rights.

At the heart of most of these **implied rights** is the right to privacy, which is not specifically protected in the Constitution. However, the court has ruled that it is implied by the Fourth, Fifth, and Fourteenth Amendments. This was the basis for its decision to legalize abortion in *Roe v. Wade* (1973).

REVIEW QUESTIONS

21. Which rights protect individuals from arbitrary acts of government?

22. Which clause within the First Amendment prohibits the government from restricting religious belief or practice?

23. Which amendment protects the accused from self-incrimination?

24. What was the original purpose of the Fourteenth Amendment's equal protection clause?

25. Which implied right was the basis of the *Roe v. Wade* decision?

Answer Key

1. The Constitution is based on reason.
2. The Enlightenment informed the ideals of the US Constitution.
3. Under the Articles of Confederation, the legislature was subordinate to the states.
4. Shays' Rebellion proved that the early US government was unable to maintain order.
5. They believed social progress was possible.
6. When writing the US Constitution, the framers hoped to balance authority and liberty.
7. The term "checks and balances" refers to the ability of each branch of government to limit the power of the other branches.
8. Judicial review is the process by which the judicial branch determines the constitutionality of laws.
9. Under federalism, state and federal governments divide up responsibilities.
10. The federal government exerts influence over state laws by offering grant-in-aid with legal stipulations.
11. Enumerated powers are powers granted to the federal government only.
12. The elastic clause grants Congress the right to "make all laws necessary and proper" for carrying out other powers.
13. Implied powers refer to powers that are not listed in the Constitution.
14. Reserved powers are powers held by the states through the Tenth Amendment.
15. Some concurrent powers include the power to tax and the power to establish courts.
16. Congress and state legislatures can propose amendments to the Constitution.
17. They believed individual liberty had to be explicitly protected from federal intervention.
18. The US Constitution has twenty-seven amendments.
19. An executive action allows the president to bypass Congress.
20. Section 9 of the Constitution lists what Congress cannot do (prohibited powers).
21. Civil liberties protect individuals from arbitrary acts of government.
22. The establishment clause prohibits the government from restricting religious belief or practice.
23. The Fifth Amendment protects the accused from self-incrimination.

24. The Fourteenth Amendment's equal protection clause was originally intended to ensure equal treatment of African Americans under the law after the abolishment of slavery.

25. The basis of the *Roe v. Wade* decision was the right to privacy.

2 The Legislative Branch

The Legislative Branch

At the writing of the Constitution, the branch of the federal government endowed with the most power was the legislative branch. Simply called **Congress**, this branch is composed of a bicameral legislature (two houses). Based on the British model, most colonies—and then states—had bicameral legislatures with an upper and lower house. While this structure was not originally adopted under the Articles of Confederation, the framers chose it when reorganizing the government. This was in large part due to a dispute at the convention over the structure of the legislative body—specifically the voting power of each state.

State Representation in Congress

Small states advocated equal representation, with each state having the same number of representatives, each with one vote. Called the **New Jersey Plan,** this plan distributed decision-making power equally between the states, regardless of land mass or population. The more populous states found this system to be unfair. Instead, they argued for a plan called the **Virginia Plan**, based on **proportional representation**. Each state would be assigned a number of representatives based on its population (enslaved people deprived of their rights would even be counted among the population, benefiting those states with large slave populations). In the end, the **Great Compromise** was reached. There would be two houses: the **House of Representatives** (the lower house) would have proportional representation, and the **Senate** (the upper house) would have equal representation.

This system had two other advantages. The House of Representatives would also be directly elected by the people, and the Senate by the state legislatures. This supported the federal structure of the government: one house would serve the needs of the people directly, and the other would serve the needs of the states. Also, it curbed federal power by fragmenting it and slowing down the legislative process.

Constitutional Powers of Congress

The structure and powers of Congress are outlined in Article I of the Constitution. As the most representative branch of government, the legislative branch was also designed to be the most powerful. Hence, it has the most expressed powers in the Constitution. Section Eight contains eighteen clauses listing specific powers which can be divided into peacetime powers and war powers:

TABLE 2.1. Powers of Congress Under Article I, Section 8 of the Constitution

CLAUSE	PEACETIME POWERS	CLAUSE	WAR POWERS
1	To establish and collect taxes, duties, and excises	11	To declare war; to make laws regarding people captured on land and water
2	To borrow money	12	To raise and support armies
3	To regulate foreign and interstate commerce	13	To provide and maintain a navy
4	To create naturalization laws; to create bankruptcy laws	14	To make laws governing land and naval forces
5	To coin money and regulate its value; regulate weights and measures	15	To provide for summoning the militia to execute federal laws, suppress uprisings, and repel invasions
6	To punish counterfeiters of federal money	16	To provide for organizing, arming, and disciplining the militia and governing it when in the service of the Union
7	To establish post offices and roads		
8	To grant patents and copyrights		
9	To create federal courts below the Supreme Court		
10	To define and punish crimes at sea; define violations of international law		
17	To exercise exclusive jurisdiction over Washington, DC, and other federal properties		
18	To make all laws necessary and proper to the execution of the other expressed powers **(elastic clause)**		

REVIEW QUESTIONS

1. How many representatives would each state have in Congress under the New Jersey Plan?

2. What is meant by "proportional representation" as laid out in the Virginia Plan?

3. What did the Great Compromise do?

4. Who was to elect the Senate under the Great Compromise?

5. Why does Congress have more expressed powers than the other branches of government per the Constitution?

The House of Representatives

The **House of Representatives** is the house which was designed to directly represent the people, and it was originally the only part of the federal government that was directly elected by the citizens. It is the larger of the houses with the number of representatives from each state based on the state's population (**proportional representation**).

Figure 2.1. The House Chamber

THE LEGISLATIVE BRANCH 19

Apportionment

Every state is guaranteed at least one representative. Apportionment of representatives is based on the census, so seats are reapportioned every ten years with the new census.

At the Constitutional Convention, Southern states argued that their (non-voting) slave population should count toward their overall population, therefore entitling them to more representatives. Northern states with few slaves disagreed. This issue was settled with the **Three-Fifths Compromise**, which declared that each slave would be counted as three-fifths of a person for the purpose of the census. Women, who could not vote until the ratification of the Nineteenth Amendment, were also counted in the census.

The size of the House grew every ten years along with the population of the United States until 1929, when Congress set the number at 435 voting representatives where it has remained since. Today, each member of Congress represents approximately 700,000 people. Residents of Washington, DC, and US territories (Guam, American Samoa, and the US Virgin Islands) are represented by non-voting observers. Puerto Rico is represented by a resident commissioner.

Each state legislature divides its state into essentially equally populated congressional districts. This process can often become quite political, with political parties attempting to draw the lines to ensure the maximum number of seats for their party. This is called **gerrymandering**. The Supreme Court has made several rulings to limit gerrymandering, including requiring each district to have equal population and contiguous or connected lines. It is also unconstitutional to draw lines based solely on race.

Qualifications

Members of the House of Representatives are elected for two-year terms in an effort to keep them beholden to the people and to more closely follow public opinion. The Constitution lays out basic requirements for membership to the House. In order to qualify, candidates must be at least twenty-five years old, have been a US citizen for at least seven years, and live in the state they are representing at the time of the election.

The leader of the House is called the **Speaker of the House**. He or she is the leader of the majority party in the House.

Specific Powers

Although it is technically considered the lower house, the House of Representatives possesses unique powers.

All **revenue** bills must start in the house. While the Senate may amend the bills, the framers wanted to keep the power of the purse in the hands of the house most beholden to the people.

The House may bring charges of **impeachment** against the president or a Supreme Court justice. Impeachment is the process by which a federal official can be officially charged with a crime. If found guilty, he or she is removed from office. This followed the British model in which the House of Commons (the lower house) had the power to impeach, and the House of Lords (upper house) heard arguments and decided. In order to impeach a president or justice, a simple majority is required. Three presidents have been tried for impeachment: Andrew Johnson, Bill Clinton, and Donald Trump.

The House must choose the president if there is no majority in the Electoral College. The House has only selected the president once: in 1824, Andrew Jackson, John Quincy Adams, and Henry Clay split the electoral vote. Jackson had the plurality (the greatest percentage), but he did not win a majority. The vote went to the House, and, after some backroom politics, they voted for John Quincy Adams, much to Jackson's dismay.

REVIEW QUESTIONS

6. How is state population determined for apportionment in the House of Representatives?

7. What was the result of the Three-Fifths Compromise?

8. How many voting representatives are there in the House?

9. What was the purpose of having representatives serve only a two-year term?

10. What TWO powers are unique to the House of Representatives?

The Senate

Apportionment

The Senate was designed to be the house of the states. To signify that no one state is more important than any other, representation in the Senate is apportioned equally, with two senators per state, making a total of 100 senators. The framers designed the Senate so that representatives were chosen by the state legislatures; there was no direct connection between the Senate and the people. However, as the power of the federal government grew, the people increasingly came to think of it as representing themselves rather than their states. Corrupt state legislatures sold Senate seats to the highest bidder rather than electing the most qualified individual. As a result, the Senate seemed disconnected from the democratic process, a millionaire's club rife with corruption.

The tension between the people's perception of their relationship to the federal government and the mechanism of Senate elections came to a head during the Progressive Era. Political machinations led to deadlocks in state legislatures over appointments, leaving Senate seats vacant for months at a time. In 1913, the **Seventeenth Amendment** to the Constitution was ratified; it required the direct election of senators by the people of a state.

Figure 2.2. The Senate Chamber

Qualifications

As the upper house, the Senate was designed to have greater autonomy with stricter qualifications. Senators are elected for six-year terms (rather than the two-year terms of members of the House) in order to allow them time to make decisions that might not be popular but that are best for the nation. They are staggered in three groups; one group is up for election every two years. This ensures that all senators do not face re-election at the same time, allowing for more consistent governance.

To be a senator, candidates must be at least thirty years old, have been a citizen of the United States for nine years, and—at the time of the election—live in the state they will represent. The president of the Senate is the US vice president. However, he or she only has the power to vote in the case of a tie. The vice president is often absent from the Senate, in which case the **president pro tempore** presides. He or she is generally the longest-serving member of the Senate.

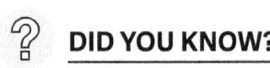 **DID YOU KNOW?**

The House of Representatives is the house of the people, and the Senate is the house of the states. In order to protect state sovereignty, the federal government was designed to serve the states, the states to serve the people. That is why the Senate is the upper house and has stricter requirements.

Specific Powers

Much like the House, the Senate has certain unique powers.

Impeachment: Whereas the House has the power to impeach, the Senate acts as the jury in the impeachment of a president and determines their guilt. To remove, or oust, a president from office, the Senate must vote two-thirds in favor. This has never happened in American history; Andrew Johnson's removal failed by one vote.

Approving Executive Appointments: The Senate approves executive appointments and appointments to federal positions in the judicial system. These include, among others, members of the Supreme Court and other federal courts, the attorney general, cabinet members, and ambassadors. While the president may make appointments, no one may take one of these offices without the approval of the majority of the Senate.

Ratifying Treaties: The Senate approves, or ratifies, all treaties signed by the president. The president is in charge of foreign relations and is responsible for negotiating all treaties; however, as part of the system of checks and balances, the president requires the Senate's approval before any treaty becomes a permanent agreement.

REVIEW QUESTIONS

11. In reality, how were Senate seats being distributed by states before the Seventeenth Amendment?

12. What did the Seventeenth Amendment require?

13. Why were Senate terms set at six years?

14. Who presides over the Senate when the vice president is absent?

15. What THREE unique powers does the Senate possess?

Lawmaking

The primary function of the legislature is to write and pass laws. The process by which this is done is intentionally cumbersome and complicated. The framers of the Constitution believed that the longer the process took, the more deliberation there would be, decreasing the risk of abuse of power.

Approximately 5,000 bills are introduced in Congress each year, only 2.5 percent of which become laws. There are no restrictions on who can write a bill. In fact, most are not written by Congress, but begin either in the executive branch or are written by special interest groups. A member of Congress is required, however, to introduce the bill. With the exception of revenue bills, bills can start in either house. Since the two houses have parallel processes, the same bill often starts in both houses at the same time.

Committee

Once it is placed in the "hopper," the bill is assigned a number and sent to the appropriate committee. Committees and their subcommittees are where most of the hard work of lawmaking is actually done. Here bills are read, debated, and revised. It is also where most bills die, by either being **tabled** (put aside) in subcommittee or committee, or by being voted down.

If a bill does get voted out of committee, it goes to the floor for debate. In the House of Representatives, the powerful **Rules Committee** not only determines which bills make it to the floor for debate, but also sets time limits for debate on each bill.

Filibuster

In the Senate, debate is unlimited. This allows for a unique tactic called the **filibuster**, in which a senator or group of senators continues debate indefinitely to delay the passage of a bill. Sixty votes are needed to end a filibuster, therefore senators often attempt to gather sixty or more votes for a bill before it comes to the floor to ensure it is not filibustered.

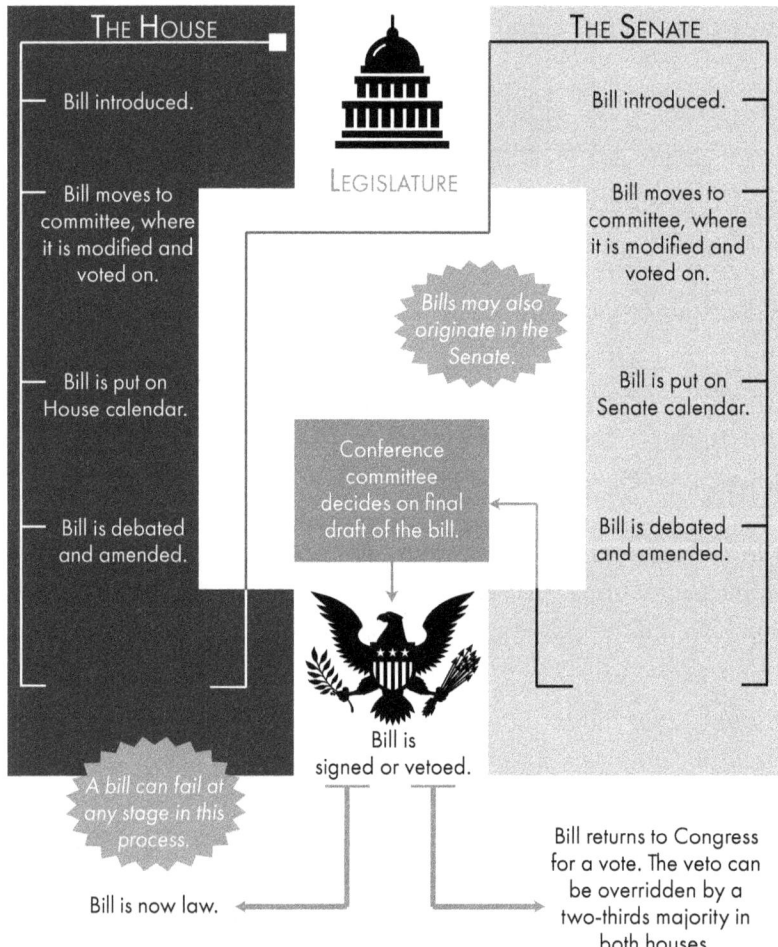

Figure 2.3. Bill to Law

Voting

After debate has ended, the members of each house vote on the bill. If it passes out of both houses, it moves to the **Conference Committee** which must transform the two very different draft bills (as different revisions and amendments were made as the bill made its way through each house) into one.

Signature or Veto

Once that is done, the unified bill returns to both houses for a final vote. If it passes, it then proceeds to the president for signature or **veto**. If the president does veto the bill, it returns to Congress where both houses can vote again. If two-thirds of each house vote in favor of the bill, Congress will override the veto and the bill will become law anyway. However, this rarely happens.

REVIEW QUESTIONS

16. Why did the framers of the Constitution make the lawmaking process cumbersome and complicated?

17. What happens to a bill in committee?

18. Why is the House Rules Committee so powerful?

19. What is required to end a filibuster?

20. What happens if a president vetoes a bill?

Answer Key

1. Under the New Jersey Plan, each state would have an equal number of representatives in Congress.

2. In the Virginia Plan, "proportional representation" meant representation in Congress based on state population.

3. It established proportional representation in the House of Representatives and equal representation in the Senate.

4. Under the Great Compromise, state legislatures would elect senators.

5. Congress was designed to be the most powerful branch of government.

6. State population is determined by a census conducted every ten years.

7. Enslaved people were counted as three-fifths of a person for the purpose of the census and for apportionment.

8. There are 435 voting representatives in the House.

9. The Founders believed that having representatives serve only a two-year term would keep them beholden to the people.

10. Only the House may introduce revenue bills or bring charges of impeachment.

11. They were being sold to the highest bidder.

12. The Seventeenth Amendment required direct election of senators by the people.

13. Senate terms are set at six years to allow senators time to make decisions that might not be popular but that are best for the nation.

14. The president pro tempore, usually the longest-serving senator, presides over the Senate in the absence of the vice president.

15. Three unique powers of the Senate include: 1) serves as jury in presidential impeachment; 2) approves executive appointments; 3) ratifies treaties.

16. They believed it would lead to more deliberation and thus a decrease in the risk of abuse of power.

17. It is read, debated, and revised; then it is tabled, voted down, or sent to the floor for debate.

18. It determines which bills make it to the floor for debate and how much time is allotted for debate on each.

19. A filibuster may be ended with sixty votes in the Senate.

20. It returns to both houses, where a two-thirds vote could override the veto.

3 The Executive and Judicial Branches

The Executive Branch

Defined by Article II of the Constitution, the executive branch enforces all federal law. Article II only provides for a president, vice president, and an unspecified number of executive departments. However, the federal government has expanded considerably over the past 225 years, in large part due to the expansion of the executive branch. Today, the executive branch is also responsible for administering a federal bureaucracy that spends $3 trillion a year and employs 2.7 million people.

Of the three mentioned, the president is the only executive role that is specifically defined in the Constitution. The president serves a term of four years and may be re-elected once. While the term length was set in the original Constitution, the term limit was added in the Twenty-Second Amendment in 1951, in response to Franklin Delano Roosevelt's four elections to the presidency (he was the first—and last—president to be elected to more than two terms). Many felt that allowing unlimited terms opened the door for a de facto dictator and threatened liberty.

Qualifications: In order to qualify for the presidency, candidates must be natural-born American citizens, at least thirty-five years old, and have resided in the United States for at least fourteen years. While the Constitution does not specifically list requirements for the vice presidency, it does state that the vice president becomes the president in case of death, resignation, or impeachment. As a result, the vice president must meet the same qualifications as the president.

The Cabinet

The **cabinet** consists of the heads of the executive departments and may advise the president on a variety of matters. It is not directly referred to at all in the Constitution. Instead, it was derived from one line in Section 2: "he may require the opinion, in writing, of the principal officer in each of the executive departments, upon any subject relating to the duties of their respective offices."

However, the cabinet as we know it today was established immediately under George Washington. He established four executive departments, so the first cabinet consisted of four positions: the Secretary of State (Thomas Jefferson), the Secretary of the Treasury (Alexander Hamilton), the Secretary of War (Henry Knox; this position is now the Secretary of Defense) and the Attorney General, or head of the Justice Department (Edmund Randolph). Over time, eleven new executive departments were added, for a total of fifteen cabinet positions. The additional eleven are:

1. Department of Interior
2. Department of Agriculture
3. Department of Commerce
4. Department of Labor
5. Department of Energy
6. Department of Education
7. Department of Housing and Urban Development
8. Department of Transportation
9. Department of Veterans Affairs
10. Department of Health and Human Services
11. Department of Homeland Security

These fifteen departments employ more than two-thirds of all federal employees.

In addition to managing their departments, the members of the cabinet are also all in the line of presidential succession as established by the Presidential Succession Act (first passed in 1792 but most recently amended in 1947).

The line of succession is as follows: following the vice president is the Speaker of the House, then the president pro tempore of the Senate, followed by each cabinet member in the order of the department's creation, beginning with the Secretary of State and ending with the Secretary of Homeland Security.

Article II is considerably shorter than Article I because the framers intended the role and powers of the president to be more limited than those of Congress. However, the president does have a number of expressed powers.

Appointment Power

One of the most significant presidential powers is the power to appoint federal officials. The president's appointment power is far-ranging and includes cabinet members, heads of independent agencies, ambassadors, and federal judges. Through this power, the president not only controls the entirety of the executive branch as well as foreign policy, but also wields significant and long-term influence over the judicial branch. This power, however, is not unlimited. Based on the advise and consent clause of the Constitution, the Senate must approve all presidential appointments. The president does have the power to remove any of his or her appointees from office—with the exception of judges—without Senate approval.

Commander in Chief

The first line of section 2 of Article II declares the president commander in chief of the army and navy. In this role, the president is the supreme leader of US military forces. He or she can deploy troops and dictate military policy. However, this power is checked as well. While the president controls the military, Congress retains the power to declare war. Presidents have circumvented this check in the past, however, by deploying troops without requesting a formal declaration of war. In the twentieth century, this happened most notably in the Vietnam War, which was never officially declared. In 1964, Congress passed the Gulf of Tonkin Resolution in response to the perceived attack on an American ship in the Gulf of Tonkin. The resolution essentially gave the president a blank check for military action in Vietnam, which led to a rapid and massive escalation of US military spending and troops. Because of this, in 1974 Congress passed the War Powers Resolution; this resolution requires the president to inform Congress within forty-eight hours of a troop deployment and restricts deployment unsupported by congressional authorization to sixty days.

Diplomat-in-Chief

The president is also considered the chief diplomat of the United States. In this capacity, the president has the power to recognize other nations, receive ambassadors, and negotiate treaties. However, any treaties negotiated by the president must be approved by the Senate before taking effect. Many of the president's diplomatic powers are informal.

In the twentieth century, the US became a superpower, transforming the role of the president into that of a world leader as well as the leader of the nation. As a result, the president is now expected to manage international crises, negotiate executive agreements with other countries, and monitor and maintain confidential information related to the security of the nation and to the rest of the world.

Judicial Powers

While the executive and judicial branches are quite separate, the president has powers intended to check the power of the judicial branch. Primarily, this is the power to appoint federal judges. The president may also grant pardons and reprieves for individuals convicted of federal crimes. The purpose of this is to provide a final option for those who have been unfairly convicted. This is one of the president's more controversial powers, as pardons are often seen to be politically motivated or a tool for those with political or personal connections.

The number of pardons granted by presidents has fluctuated over time with Woodrow Wilson granting the most: 2,480. In recent years, presidents have issued fewer than one hundred pardons per president.

Legislative Powers

Like the judicial branch, the president is constitutionally accorded some legislative powers in order to limit the powers of the legislative branch. All laws that are passed end up on the president's desk. He or she has the choice to either sign the bill—in which case it becomes a law—or to **veto** the bill. The president's veto prevents the bill from becoming law (unless Congress overrides the veto as discussed earlier). The president is required to either fully accept or fully reject a bill; he or she may not veto only sections of it. This is called a **line-item veto**, and the Supreme Court declared it unconstitutional in 1996.

If the president does not wish to take such a clear stand on a bill, he or she can also simply ignore it. If the president does nothing for ten days, the bill automatically becomes law, even without a signature. If, however, there are less than ten days left in Congress's session, and the president does not sign the bill, it automatically dies. This is called a **pocket veto**.

The president also has the power to convene both houses of Congress to force them to consider matters requiring urgent attention. While this is technically the extent of the president's legislative powers, in reality the position has a much greater legislative impact. The president sets the policy agenda both as the leader of his or her party and through the **State of the Union** address. Section 3 of Article II states, "He [or she] shall from time to time give to the Congress information of the state of the union, and recommend to their consideration such measures as he [or she] shall judge necessary and expedient." This has evolved into an annual formalized address to Congress in which the president lays out executive legislative priorities.

Many bills originate in the executive branch, either from the president's office or from one of the executive departments. The president also often uses the power of the veto to influence legislation. By threatening to veto, the president can force changes to bills that align more with her or his political agenda.

REVIEW QUESTIONS

1. Why was the Twenty-Second Amendment passed?

2. How many cabinet positions are there today?

3. Though the president is the diplomat-in-chief, what must happen before any treaties he or she negotiates can take effect?

4. What was the result of the Supreme Court's 1996 decision about the line-item veto?

5. What is the State of the Union address?

Electing the President

Almost half of Article II is dedicated to describing the process of electing the president. The framers wanted to ensure the president represented all of the states and was immune from the mob rule of democracy. As a result, they created the **Electoral College.** Over the years, the political parties have expanded the process into a nine-month series of elections by various groups of people.

Primaries and Caucuses

The first step in choosing a president is selecting the candidates. Originally, this was done in smoke-filled back rooms; it then became the provenance of party caucuses and then conventions, eventually evolving into the current system of primaries and caucuses. In a **primary** election, members of a political party in a state vote at a polling place for whom they believe is the best candidate for their party. In ten states, a **caucus** system is used, in which members of a party in a state gather together at party meetings and vote for the candidate using raised hands or by gathering in groups.

National Nominating Convention

Then, in July of the election year, the party holds a national nominating convention. Historically, this is where the candidate was chosen after days of heated debate and dealings. However, because of the primary and caucus systems, delegates at the convention arrive already knowing whom their state supports. The delegates vote for the candidate who won their primary or caucus. The candidate with the most votes becomes the party's nominee.

HELPFUL HINT

Presidential elections are held nationwide every four years on the Tuesday following the first Monday in November.

Popular Vote

Today, all American citizens over the age of eighteen are allowed to vote, but this was not always the case. The framers viewed the electorate as a small, select segment of the population. However, no voter qualifications are written into the Constitution; those were left to the states.

In 1789, in every state, only propertied white men—one in fifteen white men—were allowed to vote. Starting with the removal of property qualifications during the Jacksonian era (1830s), views of democracy began to change, and the electorate expanded. Aside from property requirements, each expansion resulted from a new amendment to the Constitution.

CONTINUE

TABLE 3.1. Constitutional Amendments Expanding Voting Rights

AMENDMENT	YEAR	PROVISION
Fifteenth	1870	All male citizens, regardless of race, are allowed to vote (though in practice, the rights of people of color were restricted).
Nineteenth	1920	Women are allowed to vote.
Twenty-Third	1961	Residents of the District of Columbia are allowed to vote in presidential elections.
Twenty-Fourth	1964	Poll taxes, which restricted Black voting rights, are prohibited.
Twenty-Sixth	1971	All citizens over the age of eighteen are allowed to vote (in most states the voting age had previously been twenty-one years).

The Electoral College

While the popular vote is tallied on Election Day, it does not determine the outcome of the presidential election. That is the job of the Electoral College. The **Electoral College** is composed of electors from each state who vote for the president. Electors are apportioned based on population; the number of a state's electors is the same as its number of representatives plus its number of senators (so each state has at least three electors). In its original conception, each state selected its electors by whatever means it chose. At first, most states allowed their state legislatures to choose their electors. By the end of the 1830s, almost every state allowed for the direct election of electors.

In the January following the election, electors gather in their states to cast their votes for president. Technically, electors are not bound to vote in line with their state's popular vote. However, rarely has an elector taken advantage of this, and it has never affected the outcome of an election. Today, most states are winner-take-all, meaning the electors are expected to all vote in line with the outcome of the state's popular vote. The president must win a majority—not a plurality—of the Electoral College in order to win. This is 270 votes.

The Electoral College was designed to elect a president for a nation that was scattered and had greater regional than national loyalty. It favors small states and minority groups, giving them greater influence on the election than they would have in a direct election system. Today many people feel that the Electoral College is outdated and ill-fitting. They argue it is undemocratic, and that it gives undue importance to certain states based on their number of electoral votes. Instead, they support a direct election system.

A state's number of electors is equal to its number of representatives plus its number of senators (which is two for every state). So, every state (and Washington, DC) has at least three electoral votes. There are a total of 538 votes available.

REVIEW QUESTIONS

6. What did the framers of the Constitution want to ensure in their establishment of the Electoral College?

7. How do a primary and a caucus differ?

8. What did the framers of the Constitution believe about the American electorate?

9. How have voting rights been expanded?

10. How many electors does each state get in the Electoral College?

The Judicial Branch

The Constitution's framework for the judicial branch is the least detailed of the three branches. It is also a passive branch. Where the legislative branch creates laws, and the executive branch takes actions to enforce those laws, the judicial branch can only weigh in when an actual case is presented to it. It may not rule or make decisions based on hypotheticals. Yet this branch has grown to be at least as influential as the other two branches both in setting policy and molding the size and shape of the federal government.

Dual Court System

The United States has a complex **dual court system**. That is, each state has its own multi-part judicial system in addition to the federal one. Even though federal district courts handle over 300,000 cases a year, 97 percent of criminal cases are heard in state and local courts. While the federal courts hear more civil cases than criminal, the majority of these are still handled within the states.

Because of the federal system, state courts have **jurisdiction**—or the authority to hear a case—over most cases. Only cases that meet certain criteria (e.g., a dispute between two states, a case involving federal employees or agencies, or a violation of federal law) are heard in federal courts. Most cases also can only be **appealed**—or reviewed by a higher court—up to the state supreme court.

For the federal Supreme Court to review a state supreme court's decision, there must be an issue involving the interpretation of the federal Constitution.

Article III, the article of the Constitution which discusses the judicial branch, only details the Supreme Court. It then empowers Congress to create the rest of the judiciary, which it did beginning with the Judiciary Act of 1789.

The federal court system is composed of three levels of courts. First are the district courts. There are ninety-four district courts in the country, served by 700 judges. They handle eighty percent of all federal cases. The next level of courts are the twelve circuit courts of appeal. These courts review district court decisions and the decisions of federal regulatory agencies.

The Supreme Court

At the top is the **Supreme Court**. Sometimes called the "court of last resort," the Supreme Court reviews cases from the circuit court and from state supreme courts, and is the final arbiter of constitutionality. Decisions made by the Supreme Court establish **precedents**, rulings that guide future court decisions at all levels of the judicial system.

Figure 3.1. US Supreme Court Building

While the Constitution delineates which kinds of cases the Supreme Court may hear, its real power was established by the precedent of an early case, *Marbury v. Madison* (1803). In this case, William Marbury—citing the Judiciary Act of 1789—sought relief from the court when James Madison, Secretary of State to the newly inaugurated Thomas Jefferson, did not deliver the federal appointment Marbury was given under the previous president, John Adams. The court, under Chief Justice John Marshall, ruled that while Madison was in the wrong, the section of the Judiciary Act allowing Marbury to petition the Supreme Court was unconstitutional because it extended the jurisdiction of the court beyond the scope established in Article III. This established **judicial review**, the Supreme Court's power to determine the constitutionality of laws. This has become the most significant function of the court, and has it allowed it to shape public policy.

Nine justices serve on the Supreme Court. Appointed by the president and approved by the Senate, Supreme Court justices serve for life. They serve lifelong in order to be independent of politics, and to limit outside political influences on their decisions. Surprisingly, the Constitution does not provide any criteria for serving on the court. However, unofficial requirements do exist: justices must demonstrate competence through high level credentials or through prior experience. Today, all of the justices on the Supreme Court hold law degrees from major universities and first served in federal district or appellate courts. They also generally share policy preferences with the president who appointed them, although judicial inclinations do not always neatly align with political ones.

It is very difficult to have a case heard by the Supreme Court. The court only has **original jurisdiction** (first court to hear the case) in three situations: 1) if a case involves two or more states; 2) if a case involves the US government and state government; or 3) if a case involves the US government and foreign diplomats. All other cases come to the Supreme Court through the federal appellate courts or the state supreme courts. Appellants must request a **writ of certiorari**, an order to the lower court to send up their decision for review. The court determines its own caseload. It receives approximately 9,000 requests for writs each year but typically only accepts eighty cases.

Once a case is accepted, each party must file a brief arguing its side of the case, specifically referencing the constitutional issue in question. Other interested parties may also file **amicus briefs**, position papers supporting a particular side or argument.

Once all briefs are read, both parties present **oral arguments** in the Supreme Court. In the oral arguments, each lawyer presents an oral summary of his or her party's argument and then fields questions from the justices. Oral arguments are limited to thirty minutes per side.

Next, the justices meet in private to discuss the case and to vote. The chief justice then assigns a justice to write the **majority opinion**, a detailed explanation of the majority's decision and reasoning.

Other justices who did not vote with the majority may write **dissenting opinions**. While these have no force of law, they are a record of alternative reasoning which may be used in future cases. Sometimes justices also write **concurring opinions**, which agree with the majority's ruling, but provide different reasoning to support the decision.

 DID YOU KNOW?

Judicial activism is when judges expand the meaning of the Constitution or laws, rather than just interpret it. The Supreme Court under Earl Warren was accused of judicial activism, in part for expanding the rights of defendants.

CONTINUE

Major Supreme Court Cases

There are several significant Supreme Court cases, some of which are listed here.

TABLE 3.2. Important Supreme Court Cases

CASE NAME	RULING
Marbury v. Madison (1803)	This case established judicial review.
McCulloch v. Maryland (1819)	The court ruled that states could not tax the Bank of the United States; this ruling supported the implied powers of Congress.
Dred Scott v. Sandford (1857)	The Supreme Court ruled that enslaved persons were not citizens; it also found the Missouri Compromise unconstitutional, meaning Congress could not forbid expanding slavery to US territories.
Plessy v. Ferguson (1896)	This case established the precedent of separate but equal (segregation).
Korematsu v. US (1945)	This case determined that the internment of Japanese Americans during WWII was lawful.
Brown v. Board of Education (1954)	The Supreme Court overturned Plessy v. Ferguson; it ruled that segregation was unconstitutional.
Gideon v. Wainwright (1963)	The Supreme Court ruled that the court must provide legal counsel to poor defendants in felony cases.
Miranda v. Arizona (1966)	This ruling established that defendants must be read their due process rights before questioning.
Tinker v. Des Moines (1969)	This case established "symbolic speech" as a form of speech protected by the First Amendment.
Roe v. Wade (1973)	This case legalized abortion in the first trimester throughout the United States.
Bakke v. Regents of University of California (1978)	This case ruled that while affirmative action was constitutional, the university's quota system was not.
Citizens United v. Federal Elections Commission (2010)	The court ruled that restricting corporate donations to political campaigns was tantamount to restricting free speech; this ruling allowed the formation of influential super PACs, which can provide unlimited funding to candidates running for office.
Obergefell v. Hodges (2015)	The court ruled that same-sex marriage was legal throughout the United States.

REVIEW QUESTIONS

11. Which case established the Supreme Court's power of judicial review?

12. In what THREE situations does the Supreme Court have original jurisdiction?

13. What must be submitted by appellants in order for a lower court to send its decision to the Supreme Court?

14. What is a majority opinion?

15. Who writes dissenting opinions?

Answer Key

1. The Twenty-Second Amendment limited the presidency to two terms.

2. As of 2021, there are fifteen cabinet positions.

3. The Senate must approve any treaties negotiated by the president.

4. The president must either fully accept or fully reject a bill in total.

5. The State of the Union address is an annual formal address to Congress in which the president lays out executive and legislative priorities.

6. The framers hoped that the Electoral College would ensure that the president represented the whole state and was immune from the mob rule of democracy.

7. People vote at a polling place in a primary, but caucuses are live events where people vote with raised hands or by gathering in groups.

8. The framers believed that the electorate should be a small, select segment of the population.

9. Constitutional amendments expanded voting rights.

10. Each state receives a number of electors equal to their number of senators plus their number of congressional representatives.

11. *Marbury v. Madison* (1803) established judicial review.

12. The Supreme Court has original jurisdiction in these situations: 1) a case involving two or more states; 2) a case involving the US government and state governments; 3) a case involving the US government and foreign diplomats.

13. Appellants must submit a writ of certiorari for a lower court to send its decision to the Supreme Court.

14. A majority opinion is a detailed explanation on the Supreme Court's majority decision and reasoning.

15. Supreme Court justices who did not vote with the majority write dissenting opinions.

4 American Political Systems

Political Parties

Public Opinion

While the structure of the American government operates much as it is described in the original Constitution, a whole network of systems that support it has developed since it was written. These systems operate within the framework of the government, greatly impacting how the government functions. As the federal government has expanded and grown in power, so have these institutions.

One of the biggest influences on the American political system is **public opinion**, the public's attitude toward institutions, leaders, political issues, and events. Analysts use the extent to which individuals believe they can effect change in the political system, called **political efficacy**, as a measure of the health of a political system.

While faith in core political beliefs like liberty, equality, individualism, and democracy persists, Americans have become increasingly distrustful of government since the 1950s. As a result, there has been a steady decline in civic participation, which has led to a decline in the efficacy of government and its political systems.

Two-Party System

Although the framers envisioned a political system without political parties, by the election of 1800, two official parties existed. A **political party** is a group of citizens who work together to:

- win elections
- hold public office
- operate the government
- determine public policy

Some countries have one-party systems; others have multiple parties. Although party names and platforms have shifted over the years, the United

States has maintained a two-party system. Since 1854, our two major parties have been the **Democratic Party** and the **Republican Party**.

Democrats generally follow a liberal political ideology, while Republicans espouse a conservative ideology. The parties operate at every level of government in every state. Although many members of a party serve in elected office, political parties have their own internal organization. Parties are hierarchical: they are comprised of national leaders, followed by state chairpersons, county chairpersons, and local activists.

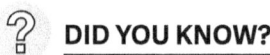

DID YOU KNOW?

The two major political parties have symbols. The Democratic Party is symbolized by a donkey, and the Republican Party is symbolized by an elephant. These symbols are said to date back to political cartoons from the nineteenth century.

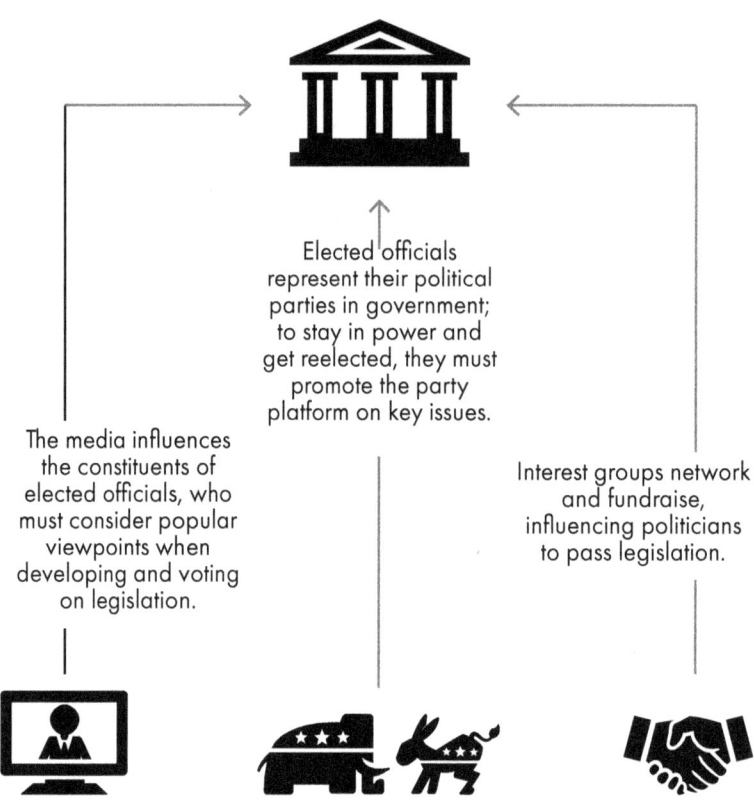

Figure 4.1. Political Influence

The parties serve an important role in the American political system, fulfilling functions that aid government operations. These include:

- recruiting and nominating candidates for office
- running political campaigns
- articulating positions on various issues
- connecting individuals and the government

In Congress, parties have become integral to the organization of both houses. The leadership of each house is based on the leadership of whichever party has the majority. The majority party also holds all of the committee chairs, assigns bills to committees, holds a majority in each committee, controls the important Rules Committee, and sets the legislative agenda.

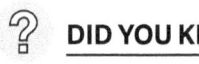

DID YOU KNOW?

The Republican Party is sometimes referred to as the GOP: the Grand Old Party.

While still very important, the power of political parties has declined dramatically since the beginning of the twentieth century. In response to the dominance and corruption of political machines, many states implemented **direct primaries** to circumvent the parties. Individual politicians can now build power without the party machinery.

Third Parties

Although the United States has a two-party system, third parties still emerge from time to time. These parties are always relatively small and come in three types:

1. **Charismatic Leadership**: These are parties that are dominated by an engaging and forceful leader. Examples include the Bull Moose Party (Teddy Roosevelt, 1912), the American Independent Party (George Wallace, 1972), and the Reform Party (Ross Perot, 1992 and 1996).

2. **Single-Issue**: These are parties organized around one defining issue. Examples include the Free Soil Party and the Know Nothing Party in the 1840s, and the Right to Life Party in the 1970s and 1980s.

3. **Ideological**: These are parties that are organized around a particular non-mainstream ideology. Examples include the Socialist Party and the Libertarian Party.

Although they rarely succeed in gaining major political office, these third parties play an important role in American politics. The two main parties tend toward the middle in an attempt to garner the majority of votes. Third parties, on the other hand, target select populations and are thus able to express strong views on controversial issues. Because their views are usually shared by the most extreme elements of one of the major parties, their stances often push the major parties into more radical or progressive (or sometimes regressive) positions. They also can affect the outcome of an election, even without winning it. By siphoning off a segment of the vote from one of the dominant parties, they can "spoil" the election for that party. For example, in the 2000 presidential election, Ralph Nader, the Green Party candidate, did not win any electoral votes. However, he drew away votes that most likely otherwise would have gone to Al Gore, contributing to George W. Bush's election.

HELPFUL HINT

Do not worry about learning the names of all of the past third parties. It is more important to understand what they do than who they are.

REVIEW QUESTIONS

1. The term "public opinion" refers to the public's attitude toward what?

2. What is political efficacy?

3. What determines leadership in both houses of Congress?

4. What did many states institute in the twentieth century to combat the dominance and corruption of political machines?

5. How can third parties affect the outcome of an election without winning it?

Interest Groups and Mass Media

What is an Interest Group?

An **interest group** is a private organization made up of individuals who share policy views on one or more issues. Organized together, the group then tries to influence public opinion to its own benefit. Interest groups play an important role in American politics. Much like political parties (and often even more directly than political parties), they connect citizens to the government. They act as a two-way street, both bringing their members' concerns and perspective to government officials and sharing information with their members about government policy. They wield more influence than the average citizen: they speak for many, and they raise money to influence policymakers, thereby influencing policy. Interest groups play an increasingly dominant role in American political life. The number of groups increased from 6,000 in 1959 to 22,000 in 2010.

Most interest groups focus on one core issue or on a set of issues and draw their membership from people interested in those issues. For example, the National Rifle Association focuses on protecting the right to gun ownership. Other organizations focus on a specific group of people, and then determine their interests based on the interests of that group. The AARP (American Association of Retired Persons) is an example of this type of interest group. It determines which issues are most relevant to senior citizens (who make up their membership), and pursues those issues. In addition, large corporations, industry organizations, agricultural groups, professional associations, and unions act as interest groups.

Lobbying

Interest groups **lobby** lawmakers to try to effect the change they wish to see. To lobby means to attempt to persuade policymakers to make a certain decision. There are about 30,000 lobbyists in Washington D.C., making $2 billion a year. It is their full-time job to advance the agenda of their interest groups. They do this by testifying before congressional committees, meeting with aides, connecting influential constituents to lawmakers, drafting legislation, and providing relevant technical information to members of Congress. When all else fails, interest groups will turn to the courts to help them achieve their goals. They write amicus briefs in Supreme Court cases or initiate court cases to challenge existing laws. They also can play a significant role in determining who is nominated to the federal courts, including the Supreme Court.

Political Action Committees

Another tool interest groups use to influence policymakers is the **political action committee**, also known as a PAC. These are committees that interest groups form with the purpose of raising money to support the campaigns of specific candidates who can further their interests. PACs are limited to contributions of $5,000 per candidate per election (it is important to note that primary elections count as separate elections). In 2010, however, the Supreme Court ruled in *Citizens United v. Federal Elections Commission* that limiting corporate donations to candidates was tantamount to limiting free speech. This controversial decision resulted in the creation of super PACs which have no limits on spending.

The role of lobbying, and most specifically PACs and super PACs, in American politics is a hotly debated one. Some political analysts are concerned that politics and money have become too closely tied together. Others argue that the sheer number of special interest groups is a benefit because they each balance each other out. In order to accomplish anything, politicians must bargain and compromise, creating solutions that are ultimately better for more people. Others still argue that rather than creating solutions, the number of competing interests leaves politicians scared to take any action for fear that they will anger one interest group or another.

What is the Media?

Any means of communication—newspapers, magazines, radio, television, or blogs—that reaches a broad and far-reaching audience is considered part of the **mass media**.

Although certainly not a formal part of the political process, the mass media has a significant impact on American politics. It connects people to the government by providing them with inside information on its people and processes, through reports, interviews, and exposés. The media also can help set the political agenda by drawing attention to issues through its coverage.

For example, the medical treatment of veterans became a significant political issue after two lengthy exposés in the *Washington Post* on the conditions at Walter Reed Medical Center in 2007.

Media Impact

Mass media has also reshaped American campaigns. Campaigns have become more candidate-centered rather than issue-centered, as candidates now must consider their image on television and other video sources. They also have to be media savvy, making appearances on popular nightly shows and radio programs.

The need for a strong media presence is largely responsible for the increase in campaign spending, as candidates work to maintain an up-to-date web presence and spend millions of dollars on television advertising space. Candidates' lives and pasts are also more visible to the public as journalists research their backgrounds to a further extent than ever before.

In the 1960 presidential campaign, John F. Kennedy and Richard Nixon engaged in the first televised presidential debate in American history. Those who listened to it on the radio declared Nixon—who was confident in speech, but sweaty and uncomfortable on camera—the winner, while those who watched it on television saw the suave and image-savvy Kennedy as the victor. Many credit this debate for Kennedy's eventual win, demonstrating the new importance of crafting a public image for politicians.

REVIEW QUESTIONS

6. What is an interest group?

7. What does it mean to lobby?

8. What is the purpose of political action committees?

9. What is meant by mass media?

10. How has the growing role of mass media led to the increase in campaign spending?

Answer Key

1. "Public opinion" means the public's attitude toward institutions, leaders, political issues, and events.

2. Political efficacy is the extent to which individuals believe they can effect change in the political system.

3. The political party that has the majority determines leadership in both houses of Congress.

4. Direct primaries were instituted to fight the dominance and corruption of political parties.

5. Third parties may siphon off a segment of the vote from the dominant parties.

6. An interest group is a private organization made up of individuals who share policy views on one or more issues.

7. Lobbying is an attempt to persuade policymakers to make a certain decision.

8. Political action committees raise money to support the campaigns of specific candidates who support their interests.

9. Mass media refers to any means of communication that reaches a broad and far-reaching audience.

10. Candidates must work to maintain an up-to-date web presence and spend millions on television advertising space.

PART 2: United States History

5 Early North America

North America Before European Contact

Northeastern Societies

Before European colonization, diverse Native American societies controlled the continent. They would later come into economic and diplomatic contact, and military conflict, with European colonizers and United States forces and settlers. Major civilizations that would play an important and ongoing role in North American history included the **Iroquois** and **Algonquin** in the Northeast. The Iroquois in particular were known for innovative agricultural and architectural techniques, including the construction of longhouses and the farming of maize. The Iroquois farmed according to the *three sisters* tradition, farming maize, beans, and squash; these plants complement each other, providing natural protection from pests and the elements, and increasing availability of nitrogen necessary for growth. Both of those tribes would also be important allies of the English and French, respectively, in future conflicts, in that part of the continent.

The Iroquois actually consisted of five tribes. According to tradition, before

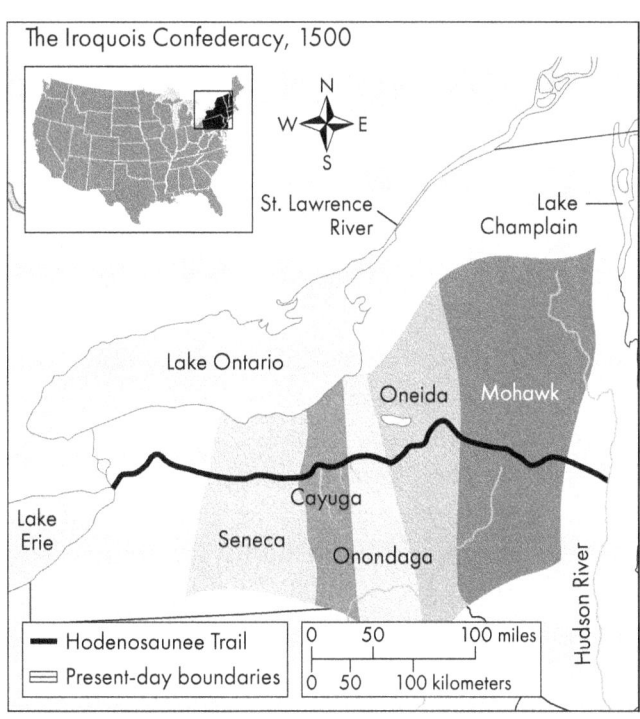

Figure 5.1. Iroquois Confederacy

European contact, five tribes—the **Mohawk**, **Seneca**, **Cayuga**, **Oneida**, and **Onondaga**—made peace thanks to the leadership of the peacemaker **Hiawatha**. Also known as the Five Nations, they organized into the regionally powerful Iroquois Confederacy, bringing stability to the eastern Great Lakes region including Upstate New York, Southern Ontario, and parts of Quebec and the Midwest. Later, the Tuscarora tribe would join, and the union became known as the **Six Nations**.

While many Native American, or First Nations, people speak variants of the Algonquin language, the **Algonquin** people themselves have historically been a majority in what is today Quebec and the Great Lakes region. Active in the fur trade, the Algonquin developed important relationships with French colonizers and a rivalry with the Iroquois. Many Algonquin in French-controlled North America converted to Christianity.

The Midwest

Later, the young United States would come into conflict with the Shawnee, Lenape, Kickapoo, Miami, and other tribes in the Midwestern region of Ohio, Illinois, Indiana, and Michigan in early western expansion. These tribes formed the Northwest Confederacy to fight the United States, developments discussed in more detail in later sections.

The **Shawnee** were an Algonquin-speaking people based in the Ohio Valley; however their presence extended as far east and south as the present-day Carolinas and Georgia. While socially organized under a matrilineal system, the Shawnee had male kings and only men could inherit property. The Lenape, also a matrilineal society, originally lived in what is today southern New Jersey and the Delaware Valley (but were later driven west by colonization). Also Algonquin-speaking, the **Lenape** were considered by the Shawnee to be their "grandfathers" and thus accorded respect. Another Algonquin-speaking tribe, the **Kickapoo** were originally from the Great Lakes region but would move throughout present-day Indiana and Wisconsin. The **Miami**, also Algonquin-speaking, moved from Wisconsin to the Ohio Valley region forming settled societies and farming maize. They also took part in the fur trade as it developed during European colonial times.

The Southeast

In the South, major tribes included the **Chickasaw** and **Choctaw**, the descendants of the **Mississippi Mound Builders** or Mississippian cultures, societies that built mounds from around 2,100 to 1,800 years ago as burial tombs or the bases for temples. Both tribes were organized in clans along matrilineal lines, and both spoke languages of the Muskogean family. The Chickasaw were a settled tribe originally based in what is today northern Mississippi and Alabama and western Kentucky and Tennessee. Like the Iroquois, they farmed in the sustainable three sisters tradition. The Choctaw, whose origins trace to Mississippi, Louisiana, Alabama, and Florida, spoke a similar language to the Chickasaw. These two tribes would later form alliances with the British and French, fighting proxy wars on their behalf.

Figure 5.2. Mississippi Mounds

The **Creek**, or **Muscogee**, also descended from the Mississippian peoples, originated in modern Alabama, Georgia, South Carolina, and Florida. Speaking a language similar to those of the Chickasaw and Choctaw, the Creek would later participate in an alliance with these and other tribes—the Muscogee Confederacy—to engage the United States, which threatened tribal sovereignty.

Unlike the Chickasaw, Choctaw, and Creek, the **Cherokee** spoke (and speak) a language of the Iroquoian family. It is thought that they migrated south to their homeland in present-day Georgia sometime long before European contact, where they remained until they were forcibly removed in 1832. Organized into seven clans, the Cherokee were also hunters and farmers like other tribes in the region, and would later come into contact—and conflict—with European colonizers and the United States of America.

Great Plains, Southwest, Pacific Northwest

Farther west, tribes of the Great Plains like the **Sioux**, **Cheyenne**, **Apache**, **Comanche**, and **Arapaho** would later come into conflict with American settlers as westward expansion continued. Traditionally nomadic or semi-nomadic, these tribes depended on the **buffalo** for food and materials to create clothing, tools, and domestic items; therefore they followed the herds.

While indigenous people of the Great Plains were widely known for their equestrian skill, horses were introduced by Europeans. Native American tribes living on the Great Plains did not access them until after European contact. Horseback riding facilitated the hunt; previously, hunters surrounded buffalo or frightened them off of cliffs.

In the Southwest, the **Navajo** controlled territory in present-day Arizona, New Mexico, and Utah. The Navajo were descendants of the **Ancestral Pueblo** or **Anasazi**, who had settled in the Four Corners area, engaging in three sisters agriculture and stone construction, including cliff dwellings. The Navajo also practiced pastoralism, and lived in semi-permanent wooden homes called *hogans*, the doors of which face eastward to the rising sun. The Navajo had a less hierarchical structure than other Native American societies, and engaged in fewer raids than the Apache to the north.

Figure 5.3. Ancestral Pueblo Cliff Palace

In the Pacific Northwest, fishing was a major source of sustenance, and Native American peoples created and used canoes to engage in the practice. Totem poles depicted histories. The **Coast Salish**, whose language was widely spoken throughout the region, dominated the Puget Sound and Olympic Peninsula area. Farther south, the **Chinook** controlled the coast at the Columbia River.

Ultimately, through both violent conflict and political means, Native American civilizations lost control of most of their territories and were forced onto reservations by the United States. Negotiations continue today over rights to land and opportunities and reparations for past injustices.

REVIEW QUESTIONS

1. What were the three sisters?

2. What Native American tribe was the majority in what is today Quebec and the Great Lakes region?

3. Where is the Cherokee homeland?

4. Which two animals were central to life for the tribes of the Great Plains?

5. Where did the Navajo live?

Spanish and French Colonization of North America

The Americas were quickly colonized by Europeans after Christopher Columbus first claimed them for the Spanish. The British, French, and Spanish all held territories in North America throughout the sixteenth, seventeenth, eighteenth, and nineteenth centuries.

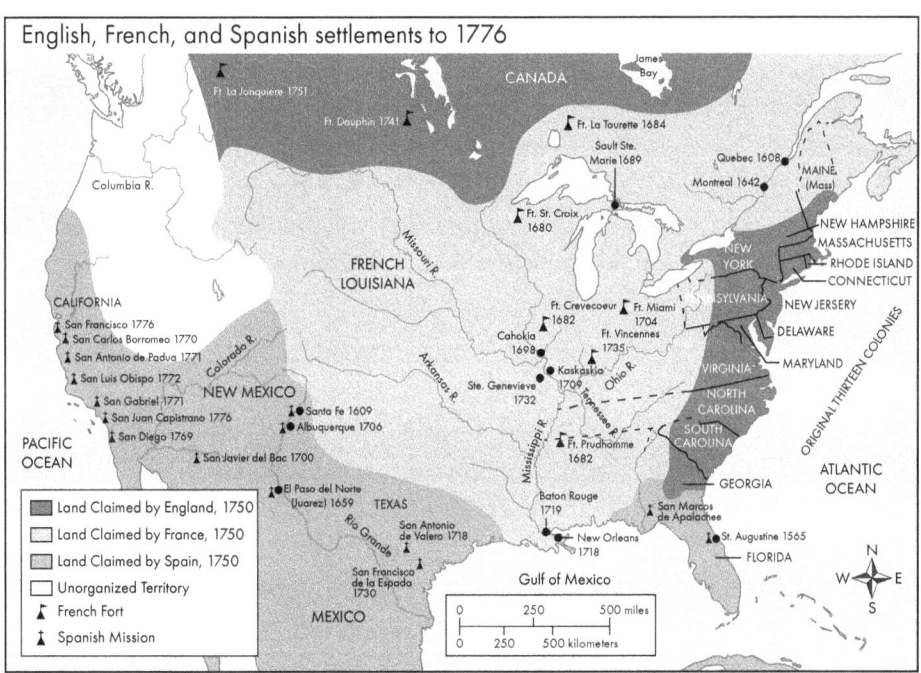

Figure 5.4. European Colonization of North America

Spain in the West and Southwest

Spanish *conquistadors* explored what is today the Southwestern United States, claiming land for Spain despite the presence of Southwestern tribes. Prominent *conquistadors* included **Hernando de Soto** and **Francisco Vasquez de Coronado**; Spanish colonization not only included the control and settlement of land but also the mission to spread Christianity. Indeed, **missions** were established in the West and Southwest for this purpose, and throughout Mexico and parts of what is today Texas, New Mexico, Arizona, and California.

The Spanish Crown granted *encomiendas*, land grants to individuals to establish settlements, allowing the holder to ranch or mine the land. *Encomiendas* allowed colonists to demand tribute and forced labor from local Native peoples, essentially enslaving them, to profit from the land.

Spain's holdings ultimately extended through Mexico into Texas, the Southwest, and California, reaching as far north into what are today parts of Montana and Wyoming. Spain also controlled the Gulf Coast, including New Orleans and Florida.

Throughout this region, Spanish colonizers encountered resistance from Native Americans. In 1680, the **Pueblo Revolt**, led by the leader **Popé**, resulted in a two-year loss of land for Spain. Sometimes referred to as part of the ongoing **Navajo Wars**, this revolt included several Native American tribes. (In the literature and in some primary sources, *pueblo* is often used interchangeably with "Indian" to refer to Native Americans; here, the term refers to Navajo, Apache, and other tribes that came together to resist Spanish hegemony in the region.) Spain eventually reconquered the territory, subjugating the peoples living in the region to colonial rule.

The conflict led to friction among Spanish thinkers over the means, and even the notion, of colonization. The priest **Bartolomé de las Casas**, appalled at the oppression of colonization, argued for the rights and humanity of Native Americans. De las Casas lived in the Americas and had first-hand experience with the brutal consequences of colonization. On the other hand, **Juan de Sepulveda**, who never left Spain, argued that the Native Americans needed the rule and "civilization" brought by Spain, justifying their treatment at the hands of colonizers.

Despite ongoing conflict between Native Americans and Spanish colonizers, there was social mixing among the people. Intermarriage and fraternization resulted in a stratified society based on race, not only in North America but throughout Spanish and Portuguese holdings in the Americas. According to the *casta* system, an individual's place in societal hierarchy was determined by his or her race, with white people most privileged. The term *mestizo* referred to people of mixed white European and Native American descent, who were more privileged than the Native American peoples.

The Spanish also introduced African people to the Americas, and North America was no exception. Forced labor and diseases like **smallpox** had decimated Native American populations in Mexico and the Southwest. Consequently, to exploit these resource-rich lands, Spanish colonizers took part in the European-driven **trans-Atlantic slave trade**. From the sixteenth to the nineteenth centuries, European colonists kidnapped people and purchased enslaved men, women, and children, mainly in West Africa. They brought African people to the Americas in horrific conditions. Those who survived were forced into slavery in mines and plantations in the Western Hemisphere.

French Hegemony from the Mississippi to the Northeast

Unlike Spain, which sought not only profit but also to settle the land and convert Native Americans to Christianity, France was mainly focused on trade. French explorers like **Samuel de Champlain** reached what is today Quebec, Vermont, upstate New York, and the eastern Great Lakes region as early as the seventeenth century. While the explorer **Jacques Cartier** had claimed New France (present-day Quebec) for France in the sixteenth century, Champlain founded Quebec City and consolidated control of France's colonies in North America in 1608.

France prioritized trade; the **fur** and beaver pelts from game plentiful in the Northeast were in great demand in Europe. French colonists were also more likely to establish agreements and intermarry with local Native Americans than other European powers; they did not establish settlements based on forced labor or arrive with families. The term *métis* described mixed-race persons; eventually France would control much of the Great Lakes and the Mississippi region through Louisiana and New Orleans, valuable trade routes.

Civilizational Contributions of Enslaved Africans

French colonizers also enslaved Africans in North America. The civilizational contributions of these Africans and their descendants to North American society were many and long-lasting. They included the introduction and production of important crops like rice and okra in the Gulf Coast area and American foods enjoyed today like peanut butter and gumbo. Enslaved Africans and Black Americans also brought traditional music to North America that would evolve into blues music (and later, jazz, rock, and hip hop). Some West African art and dances evolved into the festive practices seen today in New Orleans and Louisiana during Mardi Gras.

REVIEW QUESTIONS

6. What did the *encomienda* system grant colonizers?

7. Who led the 1680 Pueblo Revolt?

8. In the Spanish colonies, people of mixed native and European heritage were called what?

9. Why did Europeans kidnap and enslave Africans, forcing them to labor in the American colonies?

10. What are some examples of civilizational contributions of enslaved Africans?

England and the Thirteen Colonies

Virginia

While the Spanish and French arrived generally as single men for trade, who would intermarry with local inhabitants, the English brought their families and settled in North America, with the goal of establishing agricultural settlements. In the sixteenth century, Sir Walter Raleigh established the Roanoke colony in present-day Virginia; while this settlement disappeared by 1590, interest in colonization reemerged as **joint-stock companies** sought royal charters to privately develop colonies on the North American Atlantic coast. The first established colony, **Jamestown**, was also located in Virginia, which became so profitable that the Crown took it over as a colony in 1624.

The colonial leader **John Rolfe** introduced **tobacco** to Virginia farmers, which became the primary cash crop. Requiring plantation farming, Virginia required **indentured servants**, who were freed from servitude after a period of work. Some of these indentured servants were from Africa. However in 1660, the **House of Burgesses**, which governed Virginia, declared that all blacks would be lifelong slaves. The South became increasingly socially stratified, with enslaved persons, indentured servants, landowners, and other classes. The Carolinas and Georgia would also become important sources of tobacco and rice; South Carolina institutionalized slavery in North America for the next two centuries by adopting the slave codes from Barbados.

New England

While Jamestown and Virginia were populated by diverse populations of settlers, businessmen, indentured servants, and slaves, the demographics were different farther north. In New England, **Separatists**, members of the Church of England who believed it had strayed too far from its theological roots, had come to North America seeking more religious freedom.

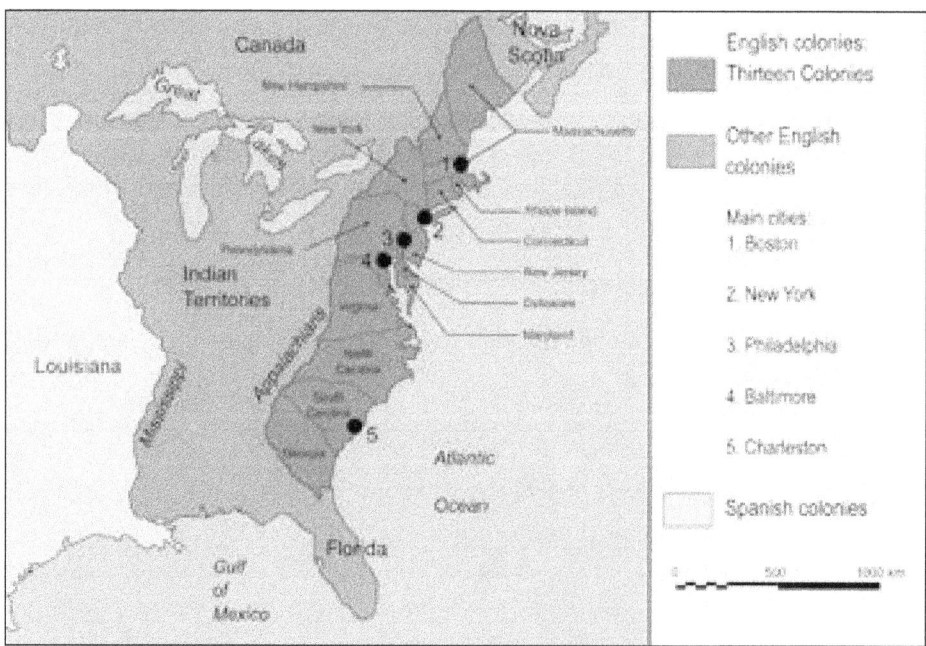

Figure 5.5. The Thirteen Colonies

The first group of Separatists, the Pilgrims, arrived on the *Mayflower* in 1620 and had drawn up the **Mayflower Compact**, guaranteeing government by the consent of the governed. The Mayflower Compact, and it's guarantee of government by the consent of the governed, was one of the documents that would go on to influence the creation and wording of the U.S. Consititution. The Pilgrims were later joined by the **Puritans**, who had been persecuted in England by King Charles I, whom many suspected of weakening the Church of England and even of plotting to restore Catholicism. The colonial Puritan leader **John Winthrop** envisioned the Massachusetts Bay Colony in the model of the biblical *City upon a Hill*, rooted in unity, peace, and what would be a free, democratic spirit; its capital was Boston. These philosophies would later inform the American Revolution.

Despite differences from the South, social stratification existed in New England as well: according to Puritan belief, wealth and success showed that one was a member of the **elect**, or privileged by God. Poorer farmers were generally tenant farmers; they did not own land and rarely made a profit.

The Mid-Atlantic

The concepts of religious tolerance were not isolated to New England. The mid-Atlantic region was well-suited for agricultural crops and trade, with fertile lands and natural harbors. The settlement of New Amsterdam, an ideal port and trading post, came under English control in 1664 and was renamed New York; in 1682, the Quaker **William Penn** founded the city of Philadelphia, based on tolerance. Penn had been given the land later called Pennsylvania by the Crown to settle a debt; Pennsylvania, New Jersey, and Delaware were founded in the Quaker spirit as part of Penn's **Holy Experiment** to develop settlements based on tolerance.

Earlier in the region, in 1649 the **Maryland Toleration Act** had ensured the political rights of all Christians there, the first law of its kind in the colonies. This was due, in part, to the influence of **Lord Baltimore**, who had been charged by Charles I to found a part of Virginia (to be called Maryland) as a Catholic haven—helping him maintain power in an England divided between Catholics and Protestants.

Triangular Trade

The North American colonial economy was part of the **Atlantic World**, taking part in the **triangular trade** between the Americas, Africa, and Europe, where enslaved people were exchanged in the Americas for raw materials shipped to Europe to be processed into goods for the benefit of the colonial powers, and sometimes exchanged for kidnapped people in Africa. In this way, North America was part of the **Columbian Exchange**, the intersection of goods and people throughout the Atlantic World.

Exploitation of colonial resources and the dynamics of the Columbian Exchange supported **mercantilism**, the prevailing economic system: European powers controlled their economies in order to increase global power. Ensuring a **balance of trade** beneficial to the mother country is essential; the country must export more than it imports. An unlimited supply of desirable goods obtainable at a low cost made this possible, and the colonies offered just that. In this way, European powers would be able to maintain their reserves of gold and silver rather than spending them on imports. Furthermore, those countries that obtained access to more gold and silver—notably, Spain, which gained control of mines in Central America and Mexico—exponentially increased their wealth, dramatically changing the balance of economic power in Europe. Long-term consequences included the decline of feudalism and the rise of capitalism.

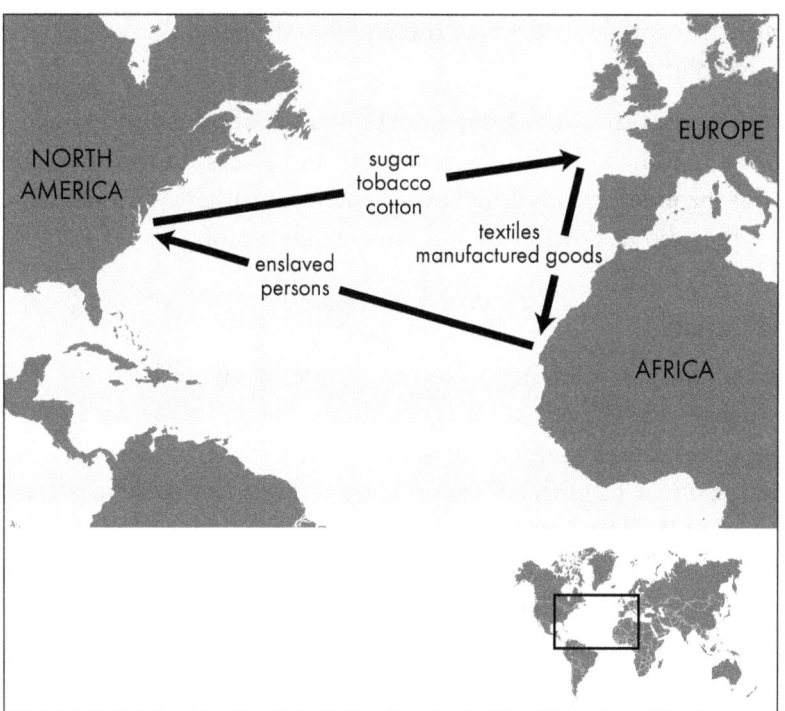

Figure 5.6. Triangular Trade in the Atlantic World

REVIEW QUESTIONS

11. How did British colonization contrast with that of Spain and France?

12. When did African slavery become institutionalized in the American South?

13. What two religious separatist groups settled New England?

14. What were the three arms of triangular trade?

15. What was mercantilism?

Conflict in the Thirteen Colonies

Emerging Republicanism

Throughout the chaos in England during the **English Civil War**, policy toward the Colonies had been one of **salutary neglect**, allowing them great autonomy. However, stability in England and an emerging culture of independence in the Thirteen Colonies caught the attention of the British Crown.

To ensure that the British mercantilist system was not threatened, it passed the **Navigation Acts** in 1651 to prevent colonial trade with any other countries. An early sign of colonial discontent, **Bacon's Rebellion** in 1676 against Governor Berkeley of Virginia embodied the growing resentment of landowners, who wanted to increase their own profit rather than redirect revenue to Britain. Following the 1688 Glorious Revolution in England, many colonists thought they might gain more autonomy; however, the new leadership under William and Mary continued to limit self-rule.

American colonists were also increasingly influenced by Enlightenment thought. John Locke's *Second Treatise* was published in 1689; critical of absolute monarchy, it became popular in the Colonies. Locke's concepts of government by consent of the governed and the natural rights of persons became the bedrock of the United States government. Locke argued for **republicanism**: that the people must come together to create a government for the protection of themselves and their property, thereby giving up some of their natural rights. However, should the government overstep its bounds, the people have the right to overthrow it and replace it.

The Great Awakening

In the mid-eighteenth century, a sense of religious fervor called the **Great Awakening** spread throughout the Colonies; people became devoted to God beyond the confines of traditional Christianity, attracted to traveling preachers and convinced that they must confess sins publicly to avoid going to hell. Many universities, including some Ivy League schools, were founded during this time to train ministers; the Great Awakening helped develop a more singularly North American religious culture. It also created a divide between traditional European Christianity and emerging North American faiths.

Resource and Proxy Wars

Meanwhile, North America served also as a battleground for France and England, already in conflict in Europe and elsewhere. In the mid-seventeenth century, the Algonquin and Iroquois, allied with the French and Dutch, and English, respectively, fought the **Beaver Wars** for control over the fur trade in the northeastern part of the continent. The Iroquois would ultimately push the Shawnee and other tribes associated with the Algonquin from the Northeast and Great Lakes area farther west to present-day Wisconsin. Given the British alliance with the Iroquois, England would also refer to the Beaver Wars and Iroquois control over the Northeast (today, the Ohio Valley and Great Lakes region) to assert their own claim over this area, which was called the **Northwest Territories**.

France had come to control the vast **Louisiana Territory**, from the Ohio Valley area through the Mississippi Valley, the area down the Mississippi River to its capital of New Orleans, and as far as the reaches of the Missouri River and the Arkansas/Red River stretching west. Not only did France clash with Britain in the northern part of the continent, but the two colonial powers came into conflict in the South as well. In 1736, French forces, allied with the Choctaw, attacked the English-allied Chickasaw as part of France's attempts to strengthen its hold on the southeastern part of North America in the **Chickasaw Wars**.

Following another period of salutary neglect in the Colonies, in 1754, French and English conflict exploded once again in North America as fighting broke out in the Ohio Valley. The British government organized with North American colonial leaders to meet at Albany. **Benjamin Franklin** helped organize the defensive Albany Plan of Union and argued for this plan in his newspaper, the *Pennsylvania Gazette*, using the famous illustration *Join, or Die*. However, the Crown worried that this plan allowed for too much colonial independence, adding to tensions between the Thirteen Colonies and England.

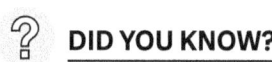

DID YOU KNOW?

After independence, Benjamin Franklin would become an important US diplomat in France.

French and Indian War

The Seven Years' War broke out in Europe in 1756; this conflict between the British and French in North America was known as the **French and Indian War**. War efforts in North America accelerated under the British leader (essentially, Prime Minister) **William Pitt the Elder**, who invested heavily in defeating the French beyond Europe.

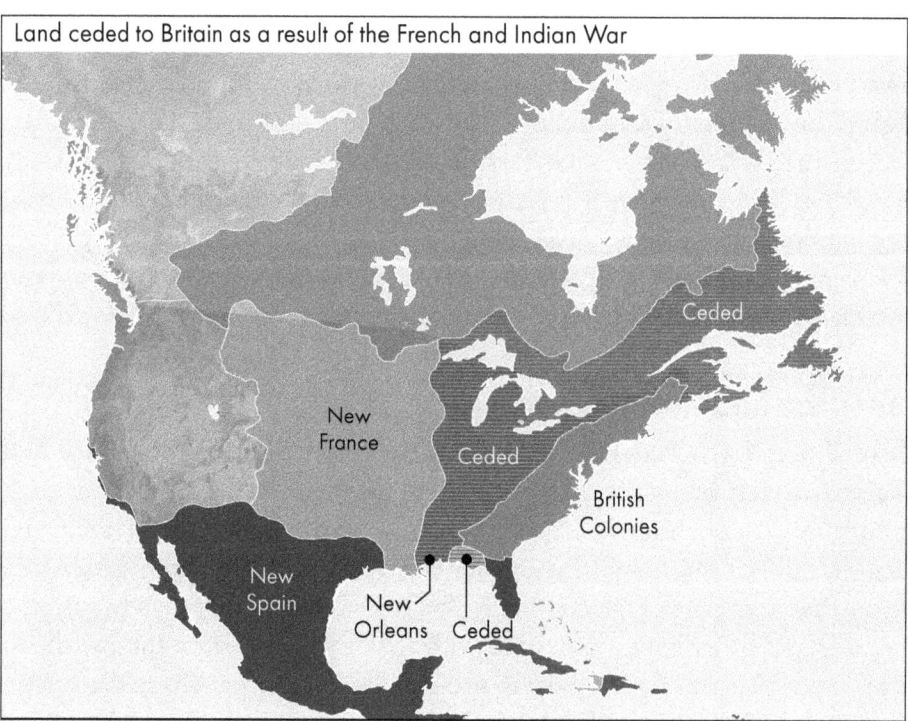

Figure 5.7. British Gains in the French and Indian War

Ultimately, Britain emerged as the dominant power on the continent. France had allied with the Algonquin, traditional rivals of the British-allied Iroquois. However, following defeats by strong colonial military leaders like George Washington and despite its strong alliances and long-term presence on the continent, France eventually surrendered. Britain gained control of French territories in North America—as well as Spanish Florida—in the 1763 **Treaty of Paris** which ended the Seven Years' War.

REVIEW QUESTIONS

16. What laws were passed in 1651 to prevent colonial trade with anyone other than England?

17. What concept of government, supported by John Locke, became popular in the American colonies?

18. What were the effects of the Great Awakening?

19. What did Benjamin Franklin argue for with his slogan "Join, or die"?

20. What was the outcome of the French and Indian War?

Answer Key

1. In indigenous agriculture, the "three sisters" were maize, squash, and beans.

2. The Algonquin was the majority in what is today Quebec and the Great Lakes region.

3. The Cherokee homeland is in present-day Georgia.

4. The buffalo, and later the horse, were essential to life for the tribes of the Great Plains.

5. The Navajo lived in *hogans* (wooden houses) in present-day Arizona, New Mexico, and Utah.

6. The *encomienda* system granted colonizers land and the right to tribute and native labor.

7. Popé led the 1680 Pueblo Revolt.

8. In the Spanish colonies, people of mixed native and European heritage were called *mestizos*.

9. European colonizers wanted slave labor to exploit the natural resources of the Western Hemisphere.

10. Rice, okra, gumbo, and blues music are just a few examples of civilizational contributions to North America from African culture.

11. The British brought families while Spanish and French colonization was mainly single men.

12. African slavery became institutionalized in the American South in 1660 by decree of the House of Burgesses.

13. Pilgrims and Puritans were the two religious separatist groups that settled New England.

14. Triangular trade included the Americas (raw goods), Africa (enslaved people), and Europe (processed goods).

15. Mercantilism was an economic system in which European powers controlled economies in their colonies.

16. The Navigation Acts prevented colonial trade with anyone other than England.

17. Republicanism, one of John Locke's ideals, became popular in the American colonies.

18. Some of the effects of the Great Awakening included: the creation of a more singular North American religious culture, and a divide between traditional European Christianity and emerging North American faiths.

19. Benjamin Franklin argued for the Albany Plan of Union with his slogan "Join, or die."

20. Britain gained control of French territories in North America and Spanish Florida after the French and Indian War.

6 Revolution and the Early United States

The American Revolution

Pontiac's Rebellion

Despite British victory in the French and Indian War, Britain had gone greatly into debt. Furthermore, there were concerns that the Colonies required a stronger military presence following **Pontiac's Rebellion** in 1763. The leader of the **Ottawa** people, Pontiac, led a revolt that extended from the Great Lakes region through the Ohio Valley to Virginia. As this land had been ceded to England from France (lacking any consultation with the native inhabitants) the Ottawa people and other Native Americans resisted further British settlement and fought back against colonial oppression. **King George III** signed the **Proclamation of 1763**, an agreement not to settle land west of the Appalachians, in an effort to make peace. However, much settlement continued in practice.

As a result of the war and subsequent unrest, Britain once again discarded its colonial policy of salutary neglect; furthermore, in desperate need of cash, the Crown sought ways to increase its revenue from the Colonies.

Taxes and Restrictions

King George III enforced heavy taxes and restrictive acts in the colonies to generate income for the Crown and punish disobedience. England expanded the **Molasses Act** of 1733, passing the **Sugar Act** in 1764 to raise revenue by taxing sugar and molasses. Sugar was produced in the British West Indies and widely consumed in the Thirteen Colonies. In 1765, Britain enforced the **Quartering Act**, requiring colonists to provide shelter to British troops stationed in the region.

The 1765 **Stamp Act**, the first direct tax on the colonists, triggered more tensions. Any document required a costly stamp, the revenue reverting to the British government. **Patrick Henry** protested the Stamp Act in the Virginia House of Burgesses; the tax was seen as a violation of colonists' rights, given that they did not have direct representation in British Parliament. In Britain, it was argued that the colonists had **virtual representation** and so the Act—and others to follow—were justified.

As a result, colonists began boycotting British goods and engaging in violent protest. **Samuel Adams** led the **Sons and Daughters of Liberty** in violent acts against tax collectors. In response, the Chancellor of the Exchequer Charles Townshend enforced the punitive **Townshend Acts** which imposed more taxes and restrictions on the colonies; customs officers were empowered to search colonists' homes for forbidden goods with **writs of assistance**. **John Dickinson's** *Letters from a Farmer in Pennsylvania* and Samuel Adams' *Massachusetts Circular Letter* argued for the repeal of the Townshend Acts (which were, indeed, repealed in 1770) and demanded *no taxation without representation*. Samuel Adams continued to stir up rebellion with his **Committees of Correspondence**, which distributed anti-British propaganda.

The Boston Massacre

Protests against the Quartering Act in Boston led to the **Boston Massacre** in 1770, when British troops fired on a crowd of protesters. By 1773, in a climate of continued unrest driven by the Committees of Correspondence, colonists protested the latest taxes on tea levied by the **Tea Act** in the famous **Boston Tea Party** by dressing as Native Americans and tossing tea off a ship in Boston Harbor. In response, the government passed the **Intolerable Acts**, closing Boston Harbor and bringing Massachusetts back under direct royal control.

Figure 6.1. "Join, or Die," a political cartoon by Benjamin Franklin

Continental Congresses

In response to the Intolerable Acts, colonial leaders met in Philadelphia at the **First Continental Congress** in 1774 and issued the *Declaration of Rights and Grievances*, presenting colonial concerns to the King, who ignored it. However, violent conflict began in 1775 at **Lexington and Concord**, when American militiamen (**minutemen**) had gathered to resist British efforts to seize weapons and arrest rebels in Concord. On June 17, 1775, the Americans fought the British at the **Battle of Bunker Hill**; despite American losses, the number of casualties the rebels inflicted caused the king to declare that the colonies were in rebellion. Troops were deployed to the colonies; the Siege of Boston began.

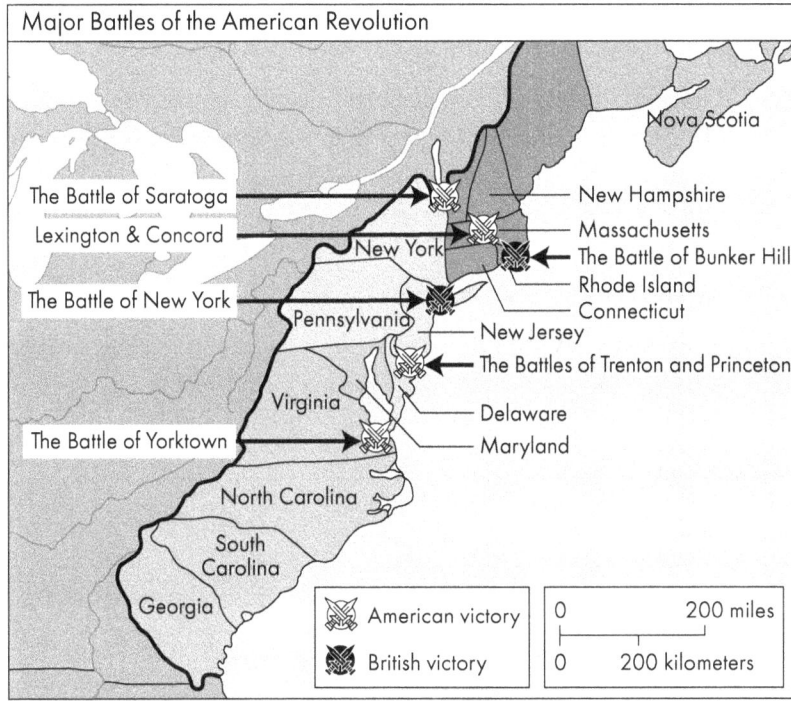

Figure 6.2. Major Battles of the American Revolution

In May 1775, the **Second Continental Congress** met at Philadelphia to debate the way forward. Debate between the wisdom of continued efforts at compromise and negotiations and declaring independence continued. The king ignored the Congress' *Declaration of the Causes and Necessities of Taking Up Arms*, which asked him to consider again the colonies' objections. He also ignored the **Olive Branch Petition** which sought compromise and an end to hostilities. **Thomas Paine** published his pamphlet *Common Sense*. Embracing John Locke's concepts of natural rights and the obligation of a people to rebel against an oppressive government, it popularized the notion of rebellion against Britain.

Independence and War

By summer of 1776, the Continental Congress agreed on the need to break from Britain. On July 4, 1776, it declared the independence of the United States of America and issued the **Declaration of Independence**. This document, drafted mainly by **Thomas Jefferson**, guaranteed Americans the right to life, liberty, and the pursuit of happiness.

Americans were still divided over independence; **Patriots** favored independence while those still loyal to Britain were known as **Tories**. **George Washington** had been appointed head of the Continental Army and led a largely unpaid and unprofessional army; despite early losses, Washington gained ground due to strong leadership, superior knowledge of the land, and support from France (and to a lesser extent, Spain and the Netherlands).

The tide turned in 1777 at **Valley Forge**, when Washington and his army lived through the bitterly cold winter and managed to overcome British military forces. The British people did not favor the war and voted the Tories out of Parliament; the incoming Whig party sought to end the war.

In the 1783 **Treaty of Paris**, the United States was recognized as an independent country. Under the treaty, the United States agreed to repay debts to British merchants and provide safety to British loyalists who wished to remain in North America. The American Revolution would go on to inspire revolution around the world.

HELPFUL HINT

Americans celebrate independence every July 4 on Independence Day.

REVIEW QUESTIONS

1. According to the Proclamation of 1763, the British agreed to what?

2. What was the first direct tax on the British colonists?

3. Who led the Committees of Correspondence that spread anti-British propaganda?

4. What TWO efforts were made by the Second Continental Congress to avoid war with Britain?

5. What were the three terms of the Treaty of Paris?

Federalists and Democratic-Republicans

Articles of Confederation

Joy in the victory over Great Britain was short-lived. Fearful of tyranny, the Second Continental Congress had provided for only a weak central government, adopting the **Articles of Confederation** to organize the Thirteen Colonies—now states—as a loosely united country. A unicameral central government had the power to wage war, negotiate treaties, and borrow money. It could not tax citizens, but could tax states. It also set parameters for westward expansion and establishing new states: the **Northwest Ordinances** of 1787 forbade slavery north of the Ohio River. Areas with 60,000 people could apply for statehood. However, it soon became clear that the Articles of Confederation were not strong enough to keep the nation united.

Shays' Rebellion

The new country was heavily in debt. Currency was weak, and taxes were high. Daniel Shays led **Shays' Rebellion**, a revolt of indebted farmers who rose up to prevent courts from seizing property in Massachusetts and to protest debtor's prisons. Furthermore, debt and disorganization made the country appear weak and vulnerable to Great Britain and Spain. If the United States were to remain one country, it needed a stronger federal government.

The Constitutional Convention

Alexander Hamilton and **James Madison** called for a **Constitutional Convention** to write a Constitution as the foundation of a stronger federal government. Madison and other **Federalists** like **John Adams** believed in **separation of powers**, republicanism, and a strong federal government.

HELPFUL HINT

James Madison is famous for being the 'Father of the Consitution' because of his involvement in writing the document, developing the Virginia Plan, and co-authoring the Federalist Papers.

To determine the exact structure of the government, delegates at the convention settled on what became known as the **Great Compromise**, a **bicameral legislature**.

Two plans had been presented: the **New Jersey Plan**, which proposed a legislature composed of an equal number of representatives from each state (which would benefit smaller states), and the **Virginia Plan**, which proposed a legislature composed of representatives proportional to the population of each state.

States with large populations of enslaved Black people accounted for those persons with the **Three-Fifths Compromise**, which counted an enslaved human being as three-fifths of a person. Enslaved people were represented in a state's population to determine that state's number of representatives in Congress, but they were not able to participate in the political process.

The states adopted both the New Jersey and Virginia Plans, creating the **House of Representatives** and the **Senate**, to represent the large and small states at the federal level.

Despite the separation of powers provided for in the Constitution, **anti-federalists** like **Thomas Jefferson** called for even more limitations on the power of the federal government. The first ten amendments to the Constitution, or the **Bill of Rights**, a list of guarantees of American freedoms, was a concession to the anti-Federalists, who would later become the **Democratic-Republican Party** (eventually, the Democratic Party).

HELPFUL HINT

George Washington served as President of the Constitutional Convention and helped draft the Constitution, leading to his famous nickname, the 'Father of Our Country'.

In order to convince the states to ratify the Constitution, Hamilton, Madison, and John Jay wrote the *Federalist Papers*, articulating the benefits of federalism. Likewise, the Bill of Rights helped convince the hesitant. In 1791, the Constitution was ratified. **George Washington** was elected president, with

John Adams serving as vice president; Washington appointed Hamilton as Secretary of the Treasury and Jefferson as Secretary of State.

Hamilton prioritized currency stabilization and repayment of debts; he also believed in establishing a national bank—the **Bank of the United States (BUS)**, which Washington signed into law in 1791. He also favored tariffs and excise (sales) taxes, which anti-federalists—who became known as **Democratic-Republicans**—vehemently opposed. In 1795, rebellion against the excise tax on whiskey broke out; the **Whiskey Rebellion** indicated unrest in the young country and was put down by militia.

Early Foreign Relations

Meanwhile, the French Revolution had begun in Europe. However, President Washington issued the **Neutrality Proclamation** in 1793. Despite this action, British and French ships accosted American ships in the Atlantic and forced American sailors into naval service (**impressments**).

John Jay attempted to reinstate neutrality; **Jay's Treaty** was unsuccessful and unpopular, only negotiating the removal of British forts in the western frontier. Furthermore, it concerned Spain, which feared changes in the balance of power on the continent. President Washington had Thomas Pickney negotiate a new treaty with Spain; providing for US rights on the Mississippi River and in the Port of New Orleans, **Pickney's Treaty** was a diplomatic success, ratified by all thirteen states. The ongoing **Northwest Indian Wars** continued conflict with the Shawnee, Lenape, Kickapoo, Miami, and other tribes in the Ohio region; the Americans gained more territory in Ohio and Indiana following the defeat of allied tribes at the **Battle of Fallen Timbers** in 1794.

Figure 6.3. Battle of Fallen Timbers

In President Washington's **Farewell Address**, he recommended the United States follow a policy of neutrality in international affairs, setting a precedent for early American history. Vice President John Adams, a Federalist, became the second president. France continued to seize American ships, so Adams sent representatives to negotiate; however, in what became known as the **XYZ Affair**, the Americans were asked for bribes in order to even meet with French officials. The insulted Americans began an undeclared conflict in the Caribbean until the **Convention of 1800** negotiated a cessation of hostilities.

Alien and Sedition Acts

During the Adams administration, the Federalists passed the harsh **Alien and Sedition Acts**. The Alien Act allowed the president to deport "enemy aliens"; it also increased the residency requirements for citizenship. The Sedition Act forbade criticism of the president or of Congress. Divisions between the Federalists and the Democratic-Republicans were deeper than ever, and the presidential elections of 1800 were tense and controversial. Nevertheless, Thomas Jefferson was elected to the presidency in 1801 in a non-violent transfer of power.

REVIEW QUESTIONS

6. Why did Daniel Shays and other farmers rebel in Shays' Rebellion?

7. What type of bicameral legislature did the Great Compromise create?

8. What document helped convince anti-federalists to adopt the Constitution?

9. What foreign policy did George Washington recommend in his farewell address?

10. What did the Sedition Act forbid?

Foundations of Westward Expansion

US Expansion Begins

Jefferson shrank the federal government. The Alien and Sedition Acts were repealed. Economic policies favored small farmers and landowners, in contrast to Federalist policies, which supported big business and cities. However, Jefferson also oversaw the **Louisiana Purchase**, which nearly doubled the size of the United States. This troubled some Democratic-Republicans, who saw this as federal overreach, but the Louisiana Purchase would be a major step forward in westward expansion.

Meriwether Lewis and **William Clark** were dispatched to explore the western frontier of the territory: Jefferson hoped to find an all-water route to the Pacific Ocean (via the Missouri River). While this route did not exist, Lewis and Clark returned with a deeper knowledge of the territory the US had come to control.

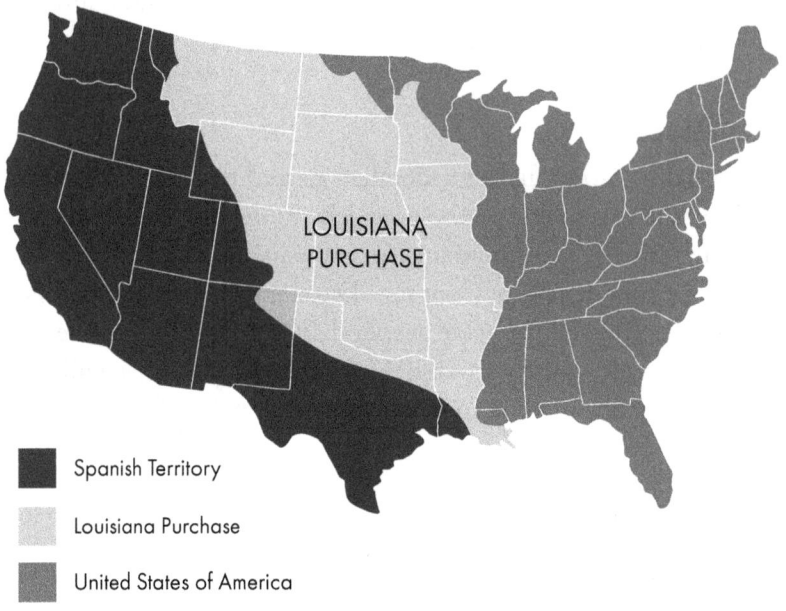

Figure 6.4. Louisiana Purchase

Jefferson was also forced to manage chaotic international affairs. Britain and France, at war with each other in the **Napoleonic Wars**, were attempting to blockade each other's international trade, threatening US ships, as the United States did business with both countries. In an attempt to avoid the conflict, Congress passed the **Embargo Act** under the Jefferson administration in 1807, which limited US international trade; however the Embargo Act only damaged the US economy further.

In addition, the United States was fighting North African pirates in the Mediterranean, who were seizing US ships. At the end of Jefferson's presidency, Congress passed the **Non-Intercourse Act**, which allowed trade with foreign countries besides Britain and France; under President **James Madison**, tensions would remain high.

War of 1812

British provocation at sea and in the northwest led to the **War of 1812**. Growing nationalism in the United States pressured Madison into pushing for war after the **Battle of Tippecanoe** in Indiana, when **General William Henry Harrison** fought the **Northwest Confederacy**, a group of tribes led by the Shawnee leader **Tecumseh**. The Shawnee, Lenape, Miami, Kickapoo, and others had come together not only out of common interest—to maintain independent territory at the northwest of the United States (present-day Indiana and region) but also because they followed Tecumseh's brother **Tenskwatawa**, who was considered a prophet.

Despite the Confederacy's alliance with Britain, the United States prevailed. Congress declared war under Madison with the intent to defend the United

States, end chaotic trade practices and treatment of Americans on the high seas, and penetrate British Canada.

The war resulted in no real gains or losses for either the Americans or the British. However, **Andrew Jackson** became a popular war hero following the Battle of New Orleans (fought two weeks after the **Treaty of Ghent** was signed, ending the war in 1814). And at the war's end, the United States had successfully defended itself as a country and reaffirmed its independence. Patriotism ran high, and westward expansion was popular.

Manifest Destiny and the Monroe Doctrine

With the Louisiana Purchase, the country had almost doubled in size. In the nineteenth century, the idea of **manifest destiny**, or the sense that it was the fate of the United States to expand westward and settle the continent, prevailed. Also in 1819, the United States purchased Florida from Spain in the **Adams-Onis Treaty**.

The **Monroe Doctrine**, James Monroe's policy that the Western Hemisphere was "closed" to any further European colonization or exploration, asserted US hegemony in the region.

Westward expansion triggered questions about the expansion of slavery, a divisive issue. Slavery was profitable for the southern states which depended on the plantation economy, but increasingly condemned in the North. Furthermore, the Second Great Awakening had fueled the **abolitionist** movement.

In debating the nature of westward expansion, the Kentucky senator **Henry Clay** worked out a compromise. The **Missouri Compromise**, also known as the **Compromise of 1820**, allowed Missouri to join the union as a slave state, but provided that any other states north of the **thirty-sixth parallel (36°30′)** would be free. Maine would also join the nation as a free state. However, more tension and compromises over the nature of slavery in the West were to come.

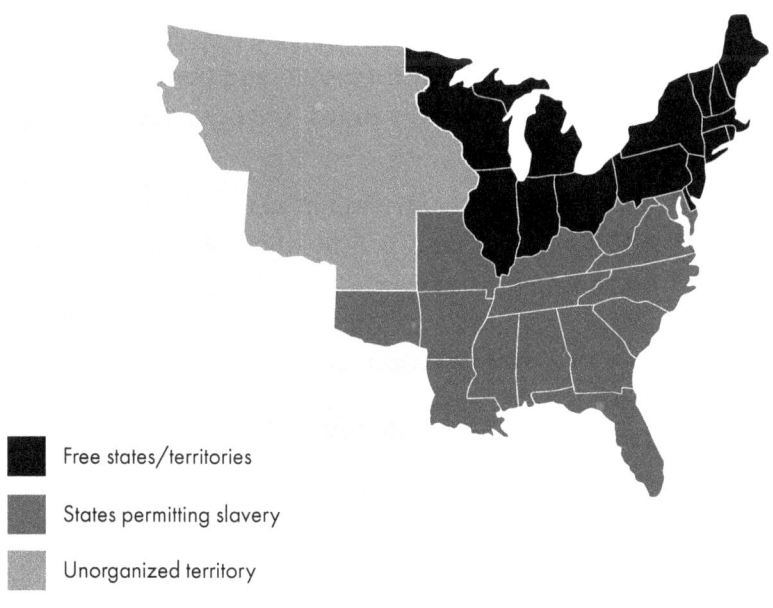

Figure 6.5. Missouri Compromise

REVIEW QUESTIONS

11. What did Meriwether Lewis and William Clark hope to find on their expedition?

    _____

12. What TWO situations led to the War of 1812?

    _____

13. In what treaty did the US purchase Florida from Spain?

    _____

14. The Monroe Doctrine closed the Western Hemisphere to what?

    _____

15. Which agreement stated that any state north of the thirty-sixth parallel would not allow slavery?

    _____

Early United States

Era of Good Feelings

The **Era of Good Feelings** began with the presidency of **James Monroe** as a strong sense of public identity and nationalism pervaded in the country. During this period, religious revival became popular and people turned from Puritanism and predestination to Baptist and Methodist faiths, among others, following revolutionary preachers and movements. This period was called the **Second Great Awakening**. In art and culture, romanticism and reform movements elevated the "common man," a trend that would continue into the presidency of Andrew Jackson.

However, not all was well. Federalists had strongly opposed the war. They had also opposed economic policies taken under Jefferson and Madison. At the **Hartford Convention**, Federalists developed an anti-Republican platform; however by the time they completed their discussions and were ready to head to Washington, the War of 1812 had already ended. The Federalists essentially collapsed afterwards.

From a financial perspective, the country would again struggle. Disagreement over the **Tariff of 1816** divided industrialists, who believed in nurturing American industry, from Southern landowners, who depended on exporting cotton and tobacco for profit. Later, following the establishment of the **Second Bank of the United States**, the **Panic of 1819** erupted when the government cut credit following overspeculation on western lands; the BUS wanted payment from state banks in hard currency, or **specie**. Western banks foreclosed on western farmers, and farmers lost their land.

Jacksonian Democracy

Demographics were changing throughout the early nineteenth century. Technological advances such as the **cotton gin** had allowed exponential increases in cotton; therefore, more persons were enslaved than ever before, bringing more urgency to the issue of slavery. In addition, **immigration** from Europe to the United States was increasing—mainly Irish Catholics and Germans. Reactionary **nativist** movements like the **Know-Nothing Party** feared the influx of non-Anglo Europeans, particularly Catholics, and discrimination was widespread, especially against the Irish. Other technological advances like the **railroads** and **steamships** were speeding up westward expansion and improving trade throughout the continent; a large-scale **market economy** was emerging. With early industrialization and changing concepts following the Second Great Awakening, women were playing a larger role in society, even though they could not vote.

Most states had extended voting rights to white men who did not own land or substantial property: **universal manhood suffrage**. Elected officials would increasingly come to better reflect the electorate, and the brash war hero Jackson was popular among the "common man."

During the election of 1824, Andrew Jackson ran against **John Quincy Adams**, Henry Clay, and William Crawford, all Republicans (from the Democratic-Republican party); John Quincy Adams won. By 1828, divisions within the party had Jackson and his supporters known as Democrats, in favor of small farmers and inhabitants of rural areas, and states' rights. Clay and his supporters became known as **National Republicans** and, later, **Whigs**, a splinter group of the Democratic-Republicans which supported business and urbanization; they also had federalist leanings. Thus the **two-party system** emerged.

Jackson's popularity with the "common man," white, male farmers and workers who felt he identified with them, and the fact that owning property was no longer a requirement to vote, gave him the advantage and a two-term presidency. Jackson rewarded his supporters, appointing them to important positions as part of the **spoils system**.

Nullification Crisis

Opposed to the Bank of the United States, he issued the **Specie Circular**, devaluing paper money and instigating the financial **Panic of 1837**. Despite his opposition to such deep federal economic control, Jackson was forced to contend with controversial tariffs. The **Tariff of 1828**, or **Tariff of Abominations**, benefitted Northern industry, but heavily affected Southern exports; Senator **John C. Calhoun** of South Carolina spoke out in favor of **nullification**, wherein he argued that a state had the right to declare a law null and void if it was harmful to that state.

Tensions increased with the **Tariff of 1832**; Calhoun and South Carolina threatened to secede if their economic interests were not protected. Jackson managed the **Nullification Crisis** without resorting to violence; paradoxically, he protected the federal government at the expense of states' rights, working out a compromise in 1833 that was more favorable to the South.

Trail of Tears

Socially and politically, white men of varying levels of economic success and education were able to have stronger political voices and more opportunities in civil society. However, Black people, Native Americans, and women were oppressed.

With continental expansion came conflict with Native Americans. Despite efforts by the Cherokee, who unsuccessfully argued for the right to their land in the Supreme Court in *Cherokee Nation v. Georgia* (1831), President Andrew Jackson enforced the 1830 **Indian Removal Act**, forcing Cherokee, Creek, Chickasaw, Choctaw, and others from their lands in the Southeast. Thousands of people were forced to travel mainly on foot, with all of their belongings, to Indian Territory (today, Oklahoma) on the infamous **Trail of Tears**, to make way for white settlers.

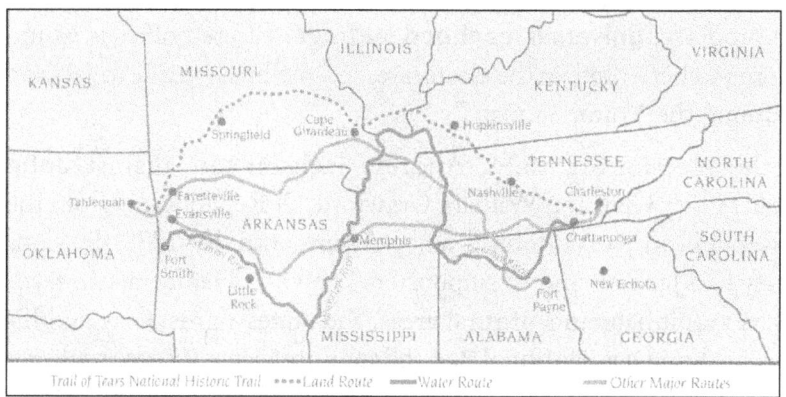

Figure 6.6. Trail of Tears

Violent conflicts would continue on the Frontier farther west between the US and the Apache, Comanche, Sioux, Arapaho, Cheyenne, and other tribes throughout the nineteenth century.

REVIEW QUESTIONS

16. What two groups were divided over the Tariff of 1816?

17. What technological advance led to more Americans enslaved than ever before?

18. What two political parties emerged during Andrew Jackson's presidency?

19. What did a state have the right to do per the notion of nullification as argued by John C. Calhoun?

20. Which North American tribe argued for the right to their land in front of the Supreme Court?

Answer Key

1. The British agreed not to settle west of the Appalachians.

2. The Stamp Act (1765) was the first direct tax on the British colonists.

3. Samuel Adams led the Committees of Correspondence.

4. The Second Continental Congress tried to avoid war with Britain by issuing the Declaration of the Causes and Necessities of Taking Up Arms, and the Olive Branch Petition.

5. The three terms of the Treaty of Paris included: 1) The US was recognized as an independent country; 2) The US had to pay debts to British merchants; 3) The US was to provide safety to British loyalists remaining in North America.

6. The purpose of Shays' Rebellion was to prevent courts from seizing property in Massachusetts and to protest debtor's prisons.

7. The Great Compromise created a bicameral legislature: one body with equal representation and one body with representation proportional to the state population.

8. The Bill of Rights helped convince anti-federalists to adopt the Constitution.

9. In his farewell address, George Washington recommended neutrality.

10. The Sedition Act forbade criticism of Congress or the president.

11. Lewis and Clark were searching for an all-water route to the Pacific Ocean.

12. British provocation at sea in the northwest and growing US nationalism led to the War of 1812.

13. In the Adams-Onis Treaty, the US bought Florida from Spain.

14. The Monroe Doctrine closed the Western Hemisphere to further European colonization or exploration.

15. The Missouri Compromise (Compromise of 1820) stated that any state north of the thirty-sixth parallel would not allow slavery.

16. Industrialists and Southern landowners were divided over the Tariff of 1816.

17. The cotton gin led to more enslaved Americans.

18. Democrats and National Republicans (Whigs) emerged during Andrew Jackson's presidency.

19. According to nullification, a state had the right to declare a law null and void if it was harmful to that state.

20. The Cherokee argued for the right to their land in front of the Supreme Court.

7 Civil War, Expansion, and Industrialization

Roots of the US Civil War

The Civil War was rooted in ongoing conflict over slavery, states' rights, and the reach of the federal government. Reform movements of the mid-nineteenth century fueled the abolitionist movement. The Missouri Compromise and the Nullification Crisis foreshadowed worsening division to come.

The Mexican-American War

In 1836, Texas, where there were a great number of white settlers, declared independence from Mexico; one reason was because Mexico abolished slavery, an institution white Texans wished to retain. In 1845, Texas joined the Union; this event, in addition to ongoing US hunger for land, triggered the **Mexican-American War**. As a result of the **Treaty of Guadalupe Hidalgo**, which ended the war following the surrender of the Mexican General Santa Ana, the United States obtained territory in the Southwest: the Utah and New Mexico Territories, and gold-rich California. The population of California would grow rapidly with the **gold rush** as prospectors in search of gold headed west to try their fortunes. However, Latinos and Latinas who had lived in the region under Mexico lost their land and were denied many of the rights that whites enjoyed—even though they had been promised US citizenship and equal rights under the Treaty. They also suffered from racial and ethnic discrimination.

Abolitionists and Suffrage

Meanwhile, social change in the Northeast and growing Midwest continued. As the market economy and early industry developed, so did an early **middle class**. Social views on the role of **women** changed; extra income allowed them to stay at home. The **Cult of Domesticity**, a popular cultural movement, encouraged women to become homemakers and focus on domestic skills.

However, women were also freed up to engage in social activism, and they were active in reform movements. Activists like **Susan B. Anthony** and **Elizabeth**

Cady Stanton worked for women's rights, including women's suffrage, culminating in the 1848 **Seneca Falls Convention** led by the **American Woman Suffrage Association**. Women were also active in the temperance movement. Organizations like the Woman's Christian Temperance Union advocated for the prohibition of alcohol, which was finally achieved with the Eighteenth Amendment, although it was later repealed with the Twenty-First.

Reform movements continued to include abolitionism, which ranged from moderate to radical. The American Colonization Society wanted to end slavery and send former slaves to Africa. **Frederick Douglass**, the writer who had himself been enslaved, advocated for abolition. An author and activist leader, Douglass publicized the movement along with the American Anti-Slavery Society and publications like Harriet Beecher Stowe's *Uncle Tom's Cabin*. The radical abolitionist **John Brown** led violent protests against slavery. Abolitionism became a key social and political issue in the mid-nineteenth century.

The industrial change in the North did not extend to the South, which continued to rely on plantations and cotton exports. Nor were the majority of demographic changes occurring in the South. Differences among the regions grew, and disputes over extending slavery into new southwestern territories obtained from Mexico continued. Another compromise was needed.

Compromise of 1850

Anti-slavery factions in Congress had attempted to halt the extension of slavery to the new territories obtained from Mexico in the 1846 **Wilmot Proviso**, but these efforts were unsuccessful. The later **Compromise of 1850** admitted the populous California as a free state and Utah and New Mexico to the Union with slavery to be decided by **popular sovereignty**, or by the residents. It also reaffirmed the **Fugitive Slave Act**, which allowed slave owners to pursue escaped slaves to free states and recapture them. It would now be a federal crime to assist escaped slaves, an unacceptable provision to many abolitionists.

Shortly thereafter, Congress passed the **Kansas-Nebraska Act of 1854** which allowed those two territories to decide slavery by popular sovereignty as well, effectively repealing the Missouri Compromise. A new party, the **Republican Party**, was formed by angered Democrats, Whigs, and others as a result; later, one of its members, Abraham Lincoln, would be elected to the presidency. Violence broke out in Kansas between pro- and anti-slavery factions in what became known as **Bleeding Kansas**.

In 1856, **Dred Scott** escaped slavery and took his case to the Supreme Court to sue for freedom. Scott had escaped to the free state of Illinois and sought to stay there. Sandford, who had enslaved him, argued that Scott should return to slavery regardless. The Court heard the case, *Scott v. Sandford*, and ruled in favor of Sandford, upholding the Fugitive Slave Act, the Kansas-Nebraska Act, and nullifying the Missouri Compromise. The Court essentially decreed that Black Americans were not entitled to rights under US citizenship.

In 1858, a series of debates between Illinois senate candidates, Republican **Abraham Lincoln** and Democrat **Stephen Douglas**, showed the deep divides in the nation over slavery and states' rights. During the **Lincoln-Douglas Debates**,

Lincoln spoke out against slavery, while Douglas supported the right of states to decide its legality on their own.

Secession

In 1860, Lincoln was elected to the presidency. Given his outspoken stance against slavery, South Carolina seceded immediately thereafter, followed by Mississippi, Alabama, Florida, Louisiana, Georgia, and Texas. They formed the Confederate States of America, or the **Confederacy**, on February 1, 1861, under the leadership of **Jefferson Davis**, a senator from Mississippi.

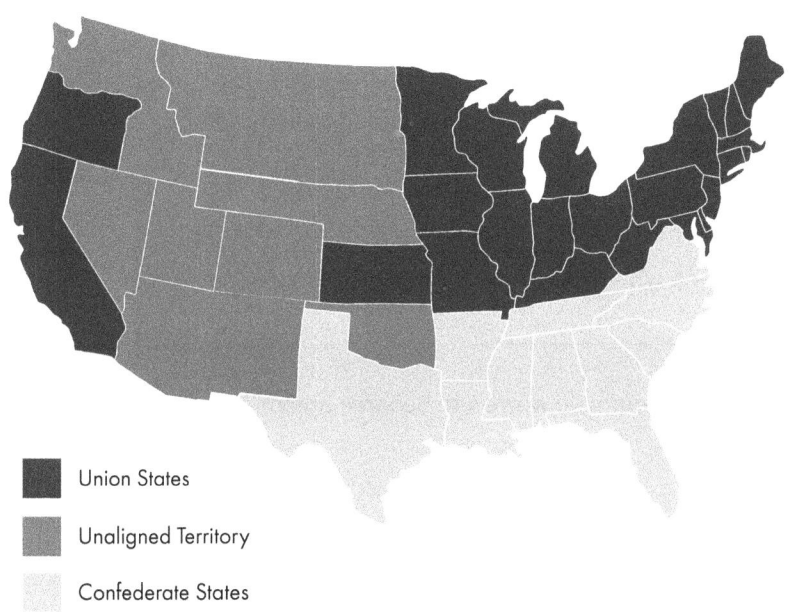

Figure 7.1. Union and Confederacy

Shortly after the South's secession, Confederate forces attacked Union troops in Charleston Harbor, South Carolina; the **Battle of Fort Sumter** sparked the Civil War. As a result, Virginia, Tennessee, North Carolina, and Arkansas seceded and joined the Confederacy. West Virginia was formed when the western part of Virginia refused to join the Confederacy.

Both sides believed the conflict would be short-lived; however, after the First Battle of Bull Run when the Union failed to rout the Confederacy, it became clear that the war would not end quickly. Realizing how difficult it would be to defeat the Confederacy, the Union developed the **Anaconda Plan**, a plan to "squeeze" the Confederacy, including a naval blockade and taking control of the Mississippi River. Since the South depended on international trade in cotton for much of its income, a naval blockade would have serious economic ramifications for the Confederacy.

However, the **Second Battle of Bull Run** was a tactical Confederate victory, led by **General Robert E. Lee** and **Stonewall Jackson**. The Union army remained intact, but the loss was a heavy blow to Union morale. The **Battle of Antietam** was the first battle to be fought on Union soil. Union General **George**

B. **McClellan** halted General Lee's invasion of Maryland, but failed to defeat Confederate forces. Undaunted, on January 1, 1863, President Lincoln decreed the end of slavery in the rebel states with the **Emancipation Proclamation**. The **Battle of Gettysburg** was a major Union victory, led by General George Meade. It was the bloodiest battle in American history up to this point; the Confederate army would not recover.

Meanwhile, following the **Siege of Vicksburg**, Mississippi, Union forces led by **General Ulysses S. Grant** gained control over the Mississippi River, completing the Anaconda Plan. The **Battle of Atlanta** was the final major battle of the Civil War; following the Union victory led by **General William T. Sherman**, the Union proceeded into the South, and the Confederacy fell. One of the final conflicts of the war, the Battle of Appomattox Court House, resulted in Confederate surrender at Appomattox, Virginia, on April 9, 1865, where General Lee surrendered to General Grant. The war ended shortly after.

REVIEW QUESTIONS

1. What TWO situations triggered the Mexican-American War?

2. What movement encouraged women to become homemakers and focus on domestic skills?

3. What agreement allowed California to enter the US as a free state and Utah and New Mexico to determine the issue of slavery by popular sovereignty?

4. What event led South Carolina and six other states to secede from the United States?

5. What was the Union's plan to "squeeze" the Confederacy through a naval blockade?

Aftermath and Reconstruction

Despite the strong leadership and vast territory of the Confederacy, a larger population (strengthened by immigration), stronger industrial capacity (including weapons-making capacity), the naval blockade of Southern trade, and superior leadership resulted in Union victory. Yet bitterness over Northern victory persisted, and President Lincoln was assassinated on April 15, 1865. Post-war **Reconstruction** would continue without his leadership.

Before his death, Lincoln had crafted the **Ten Percent Plan**: if ten percent of a Southern state's population swore allegiance to the Union, that state would be readmitted into the Union. However Lincoln's vice president, Andrew Johnson, enforced Reconstruction weakly and the white supremacist **Ku Klux Klan** emerged to intimidate and kill black people in the South; likewise, states developed the oppressive **Black Codes** to limit the rights of African Americans.

Constitutional Amendments and Reconstruction

As a result, the punitive Congress passed the **Civil Rights Act** in 1866, granting citizenship to African Americans and guaranteeing African American men the same rights as white men (later reaffirmed by the **Fourteenth Amendment**). Eventually former Confederate states also had to ratify the 1865 **Thirteenth Amendment**, which abolished slavery; the **Fourteenth Amendment**, which upheld the provisions of the Civil Rights Act; and the **Fifteenth Amendment**, which in 1870 granted African American men the right to vote. (No women, regardless of race, would receive the right to vote in federal elections until the ratification of the Nineteenth Amendment in 1920.)

Conflict over how harshly to treat the South persisted in Congress between Republicans and Democrats and in 1867, a Republican-led Congress passed the **Reconstruction Acts**, placing former Confederate states under the control of the US Army, effectively declaring martial law. While tensions and bitterness existed between Northern authorities and Southern leaders, Reconstruction did provide for modernization of Southern education systems, tax collection, and infrastructure. The **Freedmen's Bureau** was tasked with assisting freed slaves (and poor whites) in the South.

While technically enslaved African Americans had been freed, many formerly enslaved Black Americans were not aware of this news. Others still remained voluntarily or involuntarily on plantations. All enslaved Americans were eventually freed; however, few had education or skills. Furthermore, oppressive social structures remained: the **Jim Crow laws** enforced **segregation** in many states, especially the former Confederacy.

Despite the Fourteenth Amendment, the rights of African Americans were regularly violated. In 1896, the Supreme Court upheld segregation in *Plessy v. Ferguson* when a mixed-race man, Homer Plessy, was forced off a whites-only train car. When Plessy challenged the law, the Court held that segregation was, indeed, constitutional; according to the Court, *separate but equal* did still ensure equality under the law. This would remain the law until *Brown v. Board of Education* in 1954.

Black Leaders

Black leaders like **Booker T. Washington** and **W.E.B. DuBois** sought solutions. Washington believed in gradual desegregation and vocational education for African Americans, providing it at his **Tuskegee Institute**. DuBois, on the other hand, favored immediate desegregation and believed Black Americans should aim for higher education and leadership positions in society. His stance was supported by the advocacy group, the **National Association for the Advancement of Colored People (NAACP), founded in 1909**. These differing views reflected diverse positions within and beyond the African American community over its future. Furthermore, many Blacks fled the South for greater opportunities in the North, in cities, and farther West, as part of a greater demographic movement known as the **Great Migration**.

Resentment over the Reconstruction Acts never truly subsided, and military control of the South finally ended with the **Compromise of 1877**, which resolved the disputed presidential election of 1876, granting Rutherford B. Hayes the presidency, and removed troops from the South.

Settlement of the West

While the Civil War raged and during the chaotic post-war Reconstruction period, settlement of the West continued. California had already grown in population due to the gold rush. In the mid-nineteenth century, **Chinese immigrants** came in large numbers to California, in search of gold but arriving to racial discrimination instead. At the same time, however, the US was opening up trade with East Asia, thanks to **clipper ships** that made journeys across the Pacific Ocean faster and easier. Earlier in 1853, **Commodore Matthew Perry** had used "gunboat diplomacy" to force trade agreements with Japan; even earlier, the United States had signed the **Treaty of Wangxia**, a trade agreement, with Qing Dynasty China.

Despite the racism faced by Chinese immigrants, Americans of European descent were encouraged to settle the frontier. The **Homestead Act of 1862** granted 160 acres of land in the West to any settler who promised to settle and work it for a number of years; frontier life was difficult, however, as the land of the Great Plains was difficult to farm. Meanwhile, ranching and herding cattle became popular and profitable. White settlers also hunted the buffalo; mass buffalo killings threatened Native American survival.

Sioux Wars

Meanwhile, the Great Plains and Rockies were already populated with the Sioux, Cheyenne, Apache, Comanche, Arapaho, Pawnee, and others. Conflict between Native American tribes and white settlers was ongoing; the 1864 **Sand Creek Massacre** in Colorado, when US troops ambushed Cheyenne and Arapaho people, triggered even more violence. The United States came to an agreement with the Sioux in South Dakota, offering them land as part of the burgeoning **reservation** system. However, by the late nineteenth century, gold was discovered in the Black Hills of South Dakota on the **Great Sioux Reservation**.

The US reneged on its promise, encouraging exploration and seeking control over that gold. The resulting **Sioux Wars** culminated in the 1876 **Battle of Little Big Horn** and General George Custer's famous "last stand." While the US was defeated in that battle, reinforcements would later defeat the Sioux and the reservation system continued. Conflict continued as well: the **Ghost Dance Movement** united Plains tribes in a spiritual movement and in the belief that whites would eventually be driven from the land. In 1890, the military forced the Sioux to cease this ritual; the outcome was a massacre at **Wounded Knee** and the death of the Sioux chief, **Sitting Bull**.

Figure 7.2. Ogallala Sioux Ghost Dance at Pine Ridge, 1890

In 1887, the **Dawes Act** ended federal recognition of tribes, withdrew tribal land rights, and forced the sale of reservations—tribal land. It also dissolved Native American families; children were sent to boarding schools, where they were forced to abandon their cultures and assimilate to the dominant American culture.

REVIEW QUESTIONS

6. What did the Civil Rights Act of 1866 and the Fourteenth Amendment grant African American men?

7. Which court case established the notion that separate but equal was still equality under the law?

8. How did W.E.B. Dubois and Booker T. Washington differ on the issue of desegregation?

9. What innovation allowed for the opening of trade between the US and East Asia?

10. What united Native American Plains tribes in spirituality and a belief that white people would eventually be driven from the land?

The Gilded Age

Back in the Northeast, the market economy and industry were flourishing. Following the war, the **Industrial Revolution**, accelerated in the United States. The Industrial Revolution had begun on the global level with textile production in Great Britain, had been fueled in great part by supplies of Southern cotton, and was evolving in the United States with the development of heavy industry.

Second Industrial Revolution

The **Gilded Age** saw an era of rapidly growing income inequality, justified by theories like **Social Darwinism** and the **Gospel of Wealth**, which argued that the wealthy had been made rich by God and were socially more deserving of it. Much of this wealth was generated by heavy industry in what became known as the **Second Industrial Revolution** (the first being textile-driven and originating in Europe). Westward expansion required railroads; railroads required steel, and industrial production required oil: all these commodities spurred the rise of powerful companies like John D. Rockefeller's Standard Oil and Andrew Carnegie's US Steel.

The creation of **monopolies** and **trusts** helped industrial leaders consolidate their control over the entire economy; a small elite grew to hold a huge percentage of income. Monopolies let the same business leaders control the market for their own products. Business leaders in varying industries (monopolies) organized into trusts, ensuring their control over each other's industries, buying and selling from each other, and resulting in the control of the economy by a select few.

These processes were made possible thanks to **vertical** and **horizontal integration** of industries. In vertical integration, one company would dominate each step in manufacturing a good, from obtaining raw materials to shipping finished product. Horizontal integration describes the process of companies acquiring their competition, monopolizing their markets. With limited governmental controls or interference in the economy, American **capitalism**—the free market system—was becoming dominated by the elite.

Capitalism and New Imperialism

However, the elite were also powering industrial growth. Government corruption led only to weak restrictive legislation like the **Interstate Commerce Act** of 1887, which was to regulate the railroad industry, and the **Sherman Antitrust Act** (1890), which was intended to break up monopolies and trusts, in order to allow for a fairer marketplace; however, these measures would remain largely toothless until President Theodore Roosevelt's "trust-busting" administration in 1901.

Not only were products from the US market economy available in the United States; in order to continue to fuel economic growth, the United States needed more markets abroad. **New Imperialism** described the US approach to nineteenth and early twentieth century imperialism as practiced by the European powers. Rather than controlling territory, the US sought economic connections with countries around the world.

The free markets and trade of the **capitalist** economy spurred national economic and industrial growth. But the **working class**, composed largely of poor European and Chinese immigrants working in factories and building infrastructure, suffered from dangerous working conditions and other abuses. As the railroads expanded westward, white farmers suffered: they lost their land to corporate interests. In addition, Mexican Americans and Native Americans were harmed and lost land as westward expansion continued with little to no regulations on land use. Black Americans in the South, though freed from slavery, were also struggling under **sharecropping**, in which many worked the same land for the same landowners, leasing land and equipment at unreasonable rates, essentially trapped in the same conditions they had lived in before.

These harmful consequences led to the development of reform movements, social ideals, and change.

Populism and the Early Progressive Era

The **People's (Populist) Party** formed in response to corruption and industrialization injurious to farmers (later, it would also support reform in favor of the working class and oppressed groups like women and children). Farmers were suffering from crushing debt in the face of westward expansion, which destroyed their lands; they were also competing (and losing) against industrialized and mechanized farming. Groups like the **National Grange** advocated for farmers. More extreme groups like **Las Gorras Blancas** disrupted the construction of railroads altogether in efforts to protect land from corporate interests.

Farmers were also concerned about fiscal policy. In order to reduce their debt, they believed that introducing a **silver standard** would inflate crop prices by putting more money into national circulation. The **Greenback-Labor Party** was formed in an effort to introduce a silver standard. Debate would continue until the passage of the **Sherman Silver Purchase Act** in 1890, which allowed Treasury notes to be backed in both gold and silver. However, political conflict and continuing economic troubles led to the **Panic of 1893**, the result of the silver standard and of the failure of a major railroad company. **Grover Cleveland**, who had never been in favor of the silver standard, asked Congress to repeal the Act.

Meanwhile, the **Colored Farmers' Alliance** formed to support sharecroppers and other African American farmers in the South. The racist Jim Crow laws remained in place in many states, for segregation had been reaffirmed by the Supreme Court case *Plessy v. Ferguson*. The NAACP was formed to advocate for African Americans nationwide and still functions today.

The Labor Movement

At the same time, the **labor movement** emerged to support mistreated industrial workers in urban areas. **Samuel Gompers** led the **American Federation of Labor (AFL)**, using **strikes** and **collective bargaining** to gain protections for the unskilled workers who had come to cities seeking industrial jobs. The **Knights of Labor** further empowered workers by integrating unskilled workers into actions. **Mother Jones** revolutionized labor by including women, children, and African Americans into labor actions.

Poor conditions led to philosophies of reform. Many workers were inspired by **socialism**, the philosophy developed in Europe that the workers should own the means of production and that wealth should be distributed equally, taking into account strong economic planning. Other radical movements included **utopianism**, whose adherents conceptualized establishing utopian settlements with egalitarian societies. More modern philosophies included the **Social Gospel**, the notion that it was society's obligation to ensure better treatment for workers and immigrants. With the continual rise of the **middle class**, women took a more active role in advocating for the poor and for themselves. Women activists also aligned with labor and the emerging Progressive Movement.

With the Progressive **Theodore Roosevelt's** ascension to the presidency in 1901 following President William McKinley's assassination, the Progressive Era reached its apex. The *trust-buster* Roosevelt enforced the Sherman Antitrust Act and prosecuted the **Northern Securities** railroad monopoly under the Interstate Commerce Act, breaking up trusts and creating a fairer market. He led government involvement in negotiations between unions and industrial powers, developing the *square deal* for fairer treatment of workers. The Progressive Era also saw a series of acts to protect workers, health, farmers, and children under Presidents Roosevelt and Taft.

Spanish-American War

Roosevelt continued overseas expansion following McKinley's **Spanish-American War** (1898 – 1901), in which the US gained control over Spanish territory in the Caribbean, Asia, and the South Pacific.

The Spanish-American War had been the first time the United States had engaged in overseas military occupation and conquest beyond North America, entirely contrary to George Washington's recommendations in his Farewell Address.

During this period, the US annexed Hawaii, Guam, Puerto Rico, and took over the Panama Canal; Cuba became a US protectorate; and the US annexed the Philippines, which would fight an ongoing guerrilla war for independence.

Spanish abuses in Cuba had concerned Americans; however, many events were sensationalized and exaggerated in the media—this **yellow journalism** aroused popular concern and interest in intervention in Cuba. The discovery of a letter from the Spanish minister de Lome, which insulted President McKinley, along with the mysterious explosion of the USS *Maine* in Havana spurred the US into action.

Roosevelt Corollary to the Monroe Doctrine

Many Americans did not support intervention, however. According to the **Teller Amendment**, Cuba would revert to independence following the war. The US signed a peace treaty with Spain in 1898. As a result, it controlled Puerto Rico and Guam. Despite having promised independence to the Philippines, McKinley elected to keep it; furthermore, under the **Platt Amendment**, the United States effectively took over Cuba despite previous promises of independence.

The **Roosevelt Corollary** to the Monroe Doctrine, which promised US intervention in Latin America in case of European intervention there, essentially gave the US total dominance over Latin America. Under the **Hay-Pauncefote Treaty**, Great Britain granted its claims to the area that would become the Panama Canal (at the time, in Colombia) to the US.

As Colombia refused to recognize the treaty, President Roosevelt engineered a revolution, creating the new country of Panama, and beginning construction of the canal. This **new imperialism** expanded US markets and increased US presence and prestige on the global stage.

REVIEW QUESTIONS

11. What strategies did monopolies and trusts use to dominate the economy during the Gilded Age?

12. How did New Imperialism differ from other past types of imperialism?

13. What system in the South kept African Americans in conditions akin to enslavement?

14. What political party formed in response to corruption harming farmers?

15. What conflict was the first time the US engaged in overseas military occupation and conquest beyond North America?

Answer Key

1. Texas' entry into the United States and the US hunger for land triggered the Mexican-American War.

2. The Cult of Domesticity encouraged women to become homemakers and focus on domestic skills.

3. The Compromise of 1850 allowed California to enter the US as a free state and Utah and New Mexico to determine the issue of slavery by popular sovereignty.

4. After the election of Abraham Lincoln (1860), South Carolina seceded from the United States, quickly followed by six other Southern states.

5. The Anaconda Plan was the Union's plan to "squeeze" the Confederacy through a naval blockade.

6. The Civil Rights Act of 1866 and the Fourteenth Amendment granted Black American men citizenship and the same rights as white men (though this did not necessarily occur in practice).

7. *Plessy v. Ferguson* (1896) established the notion that separate but equal was still equality under the law.

8. Washington believed in gradual desegregation while Dubois believed in immediate desegregation.

9. Clipper ships helped open trans-Pacific trade (between the US and East Asia).

10. The Ghost Dance Movement was a spiritual movement that united the tribes of the Great Plains in a belief that white people would eventually be driven from the land.

11. Monopolies and trusts used vertical and horizontal integration to dominate the economy during the Gilded Age.

12. Under New Imperialism, the US sought economic connections with countries around the world rather than to control territory.

13. Sharecropping, while not technically slavery, kept many Black Americans in debt and poverty.

14. The People's Party (the Populist Party) was formed to fight corruption that harmed farmers.

15. The Spanish-American War was the first conflict in which the US engaged in overseas military occupation and conquest beyond North America.

8 The United States Becomes a Global Power

Socioeconomic Change and World War I

Progressive Era

Social change led by the Progressives in the early twentieth century resulted in better conditions for workers, increased attention toward child labor, and calls for more livable cities.

The Roosevelt administration focused its attention on economic change at the corporate level. The **Sherman Antitrust Act**, despite its intended purpose—to prosecute and dissolve large trusts and create a fairer marketplace—had actually been used against unions and farmers' alliances. Under Roosevelt, the Act was used to prosecute enormous trusts like the **Northern Securities Company**, which controlled much of the railroad industry, and **Standard Oil**. Actions like this earned Roosevelt his reputation as a trust-buster.

Continuing economic instability also triggered top-down reform. Banks restricting credit and overspeculating on the value of land and interests, coupled with a conservative gold standard, led to the **Panic of 1907**. To stabilize the economy and rein in the banks, Congress passed the **Federal Reserve Act** in 1913 to protect the banking system. Federal Reserve banks were established to cover twelve regions of the country; commercial banks had to take part in the system, allowing "the Fed" to control interest rates and avoid a similar crisis.

During the Progressive Era, while the United States became increasingly prosperous and stable, Europe was becoming increasingly unstable. Americans were divided over how to respond. Following the Spanish-American War, debate had arisen within the US between **interventionism** and **isolationism**—whether the US should intervene in international matters or not. Interventionists believed in spreading US-style democracy, while isolationists believed in focusing on development at home. This debate became more pronounced with the outbreak of World War I in Europe.

World War I

Inflammatory events like German **submarine warfare** (U-boats) in the Atlantic Ocean, the sinking of the *Lusitania*, which resulted in many American civilian deaths, the embarrassing **Zimmerman Telegram** (in which Germany promised to help Mexico in an attack on the US), and growing American **nationalism**, or pride in and identification with one's country, triggered US intervention. The US declared war in 1917. With victory in 1918, the US had proven itself a superior military and industrial power. Interventionist **President Woodrow Wilson** played an important role in negotiating the peace; his **Fourteen Points** laid out an idealistic international vision, including an international security organization. However, European powers negotiated and won the harsh **Treaty of Versailles**, which placed the blame for the war entirely on Germany and demanded crippling **reparations** from it, one contributing factor to **World War II** later in the twentieth century. The **League of Nations**, a collective security organization, was formed, but a divided US Congress refused to ratify the Treaty, so the US did not join it. Consequently, the League was weak and largely ineffective.

Isolation and Xenophobia

Divisions between interventionists and isolationists continued. Following the Japanese invasion of Manchuria in 1932, the **Stimson Doctrine** determined US neutrality in Asia. Congress also passed the **Neutrality Acts** of 1930s in face of conflict in Asia and ongoing tensions in Europe.

On the home front, fear of homegrown radicals—particularly of communists and anarchists—and xenophobia against immigrants led to the **Red Scare** in 1919 and a series of anti-immigration laws. Attorney-General Palmer authorized **J. Edgar Hoover** (who would later head the FBI) to lead a series of raids (the **Palmer Raids**) on suspected radicals, precipitating the hysteria of the Red Scare. Palmer was later discredited.

In response to widespread xenophobia and a sentiment of isolationism following the First World War, Congress limited immigration specifically from Asia, Eastern Europe, and Southern Europe with the racist **Emergency Quota Act** of 1921 and **National Origins Act** of 1924.

The Great Migration and Racism

The ongoing Great Migration of Black Americans from the South to Northern states and the West led to differing views on black empowerment. Leaders like **Marcus Garvey** believed in self-sufficiency for Black people, who were settling in urban areas and facing racial discrimination and isolation. Garvey's **United Negro Improvement Association** would go on to inspire movements like the Black Panthers and the Nation of Islam. However, those philosophies of separation were at odds with the NAACP, which supported integration.

Social tensions increased with 1919 race riots. In the South and Midwest, the Ku Klux Klan was growing in power. Black Americans faced intimidation, violence, and death. **Lynchings**, in which Black people were kidnapped and killed, sometimes publicly, occurred. Events like the Tulsa race massacre happened throughout the country.

The Roaring Twenties

Despite riots and discrimination in northern cities, Black American culture did flourish and become an integral part of growing American popular culture. The **Harlem Renaissance**, the development and popularity of African American–dominated music (especially **jazz**), literature, and art, was extremely popular nationwide and contributed to the development of American pop culture. So did the evolution of early technology like radio, motion pictures, and automobiles—products which were available to the middle class through credit. Furthermore, the women's rights movement was empowered by the heightened visibility of women in the public sphere; the **Nineteenth Amendment**, giving all women the right to vote, was ratified in 1920. However, the **Roaring Twenties**, a seemingly trouble-free period of isolation from chaotic world events, would come to an end.

 DID YOU KNOW?

White residents attacked Black people and businesses on what was known as "Black Wall Street" in the Greenwood area of Tulsa, Oklahoma, on May 31 and June 1, 1931. In what became known as the Tulsa race massacre, a young Black man was accused of assaulting a young white woman. He was arrested, and Black and white residents confronted each other over rumors that he would be lynched. Days of mob violence followed, with tacit support to white mobs provided by law enforcement. Black businesses were destroyed, and many people were killed. The Tulsa race massacre was only one of several such events in the early twentieth century.

REVIEW QUESTIONS

1. What crisis led to the establishment of the Federal Reserve?

2. How did interventionism and isolationism differ?

3. What are FOUR events that led the US to enter World War I?

4. What TWO racist acts were passed after World War I as a result of xenophobia and isolationism?

5. How did Marcus Garvey's views differ from those of the NAACP?

The Great Depression in the United States

Causes of the Great Depression

Following WWI, the United States had experienced an era of consumerism and corruption. The government sponsored **laissez-faire** policies and supported **manufacturing**, flooding markets with cheap consumer goods. Union membership suffered; so did farmers, due to falling crop prices. While mass-production helped the emerging middle class afford more consumer goods and improve their living standards, many families resorted to **credit** to fuel consumer spending. These risky consumer loans, **overspeculation** on crops and the value of farmland, and weak banking protections helped bring about the **Great Depression,** commonly dated from October 29, 1929, or *Black Tuesday*, when the stock market collapsed. During the same time period, a major drought occurred in the Great Plains, affecting farmers throughout the region. Millions of Americans faced unemployment and poverty.

Speculation, or margin-buying, meant that speculators borrowed money to buy stock, selling it as soon as its price rose. However, since the price of stocks fluctuated, when buyers lost confidence in the market and began selling their shares, the value of stocks fell. Borrowers could not repay their loans; as a result, banks failed.

Figure 8.1. Great Depression

FDR and the New Deal

Following weak responses by the Hoover administration, **Franklin Delano Roosevelt** was elected to the presidency in 1932. FDR offered Americans a *New Deal*: a plan to bring the country out of the Depression. During the *First Hundred Days* of FDR's administration, a series of emergency acts (known as an *alphabet soup* of acts due to their many acronyms) was passed for the immediate repair of the banking system. Perhaps most notable was the **Glass-Steagal Act**, which established the **Federal Deposit Insurance Corporation (FDIC)** to insure customer deposits in the wake of bank failures. (Later, to monitor stock trading, the **Securities and Exchange Commission (SEC)** was established; it also has the power to punish violators of the law.) To address the effects of overspeculation on land, the **Agricultural Adjustment Act (AAA)** reduced farm prices by subsidizing farmers to reduce production of commodities. The **Home Owners Loan Corporation (HOLC)** refinanced mortgages to protect homeowners from losing their homes, and the **Federal Housing Administration (FHA)** was created for the long term to insure low-cost mortgages.

New Deal Programs

The **Tennessee Valley Authority (TVA)** was the first large-scale attempt at regional public planning; despite being part of the First Hundred Days, it was a long-term project. While intended to create jobs and bring electricity to the impoverished rural inhabitants of the Tennessee Valley area, one of its true objectives was to accurately measure the cost of electric power, which had been supplied by private companies. The TVA was the first public power company and still operates today.

FDR did not only address economic issues; a number of acts provided relief to the poor and unemployed. The federal government allotted aid to states to be distributed directly to the poor through the **Federal Emergency Relief Act**. The New Deal especially generated jobs. The federal government distributed funding to states through the **Public Works Administration (PWA)** for the purpose of developing infrastructure and to provide construction jobs for the unemployed. Likewise, the **Civilian Conservation Corps (CCC)** offered employment in environmental conservation and management projects. Later, during the **Second New Deal**, the **Works Progress Administration (WPA)** was established. The WPA was a long-term project that generated construction jobs and built infrastructure throughout the country. It also employed writers and artists. The **Federal Writers' Project** and the **Federal Art Project** created jobs for writers and artists, who wrote histories, created guidebooks, developed public art for public buildings, and made other contributions.

The New Deal addressed labor issues as well. The **Wagner Act** ensured the right to unionize and established the **National Labor Relations Board (NLRB)**. Strengthening unions guaranteed collective bargaining rights and protected workers.

FDR was a Democrat in the Progressive tradition; the Progressive legacy of social improvement was apparent throughout the New Deal and his administration. The New Deal and its positive impact on the poor, the working class, unions, and immigrants led these groups to support the Democratic Party, a trend that continues to this day.

 DID YOU KNOW?

The Federal Writers' Project enlisted unemployed writers to interview Black Americans who had been enslaved. The outcome was a compilation, *Born in Slavery: Slave Narratives from the Federal Writers' Project, 1936–1938* that is available at the Library of Congress. These narratives are some of the few recorded histories of Black Americans who had been enslaved, in their own words and from their perspective.

REVIEW QUESTIONS

6. What event is generally considered the start of the Great Depression?

   _____

7. What did the FDIC insure customer deposits against?

   _____

8. What was the first American public power company?

9. Why was the Public Works Administration (PWA) started?

10. What TWO things did the Wagner Act do?

The United States and World War II

Cooperation with Europe

The entire world suffered from the Great Depression, and Europe became increasingly unstable. With the rise of the radical Nazi Party in Germany, the Nazi leader Adolf Hitler led German takeovers of several European countries and became a threat to US allies, bombing Britain. However, the United States, weakened by the Great Depression and reluctant to engage in international affairs due to continuing public and political support for isolationism, reinforced by the Neutrality Acts, remained militarily uncommitted in the war. However, the Neutrality Act of 1939 allowed cash-and-carry arms sales to combat participants; in this way, the United States could militarily support its allies (namely, Great Britain).

FDR was increasingly concerned about the rise of fascism in Europe, seeing it as a global threat. To ally with and support Great Britain without technically declaring war on Germany, FDR convinced Congress to enact the **Lend-Lease Act**, directly supplying Britain with military aid, in place of cash-and-carry. FDR and the British Prime Minister **Winston Churchill** met in response to the non-aggression pact between Hitler and Stalin to sign the **Atlantic Charter**, which laid out the anti-fascist agenda of free trade and self-determination. To garner support for his position, FDR spoke publicly about the **Four Freedoms**: freedom of speech, freedom of religion, freedom from want, and freedom from fear.

US Enters the War

However, after the Japanese attack on **Pearl Harbor** on December 7, 1941, the US entered the war. While directly attacked by Japan, allied with the fascist Axis powers of Italy and Germany, the United States focused first on the European theater, having agreed with the other Allied powers (Great Britain and the Soviet Union) that Hitler was the primary global threat. The United States focused on eliminating the Nazi threat in the air and at sea, destroying Nazi U-boats (submarines) that threatened the Allies throughout the Atlantic. The US also engaged Germany in North Africa, defeating its troops to approach the fascist Italy from the Mediterranean. On June 6, 1944, or **D-Day**, the US led the invasion of Normandy, invading German-controlled Europe. After months of fighting, following the deadly and drawn-out **Battle of the Bulge** when the

Allies faced fierce German resistance, the Allies were able to enter Germany and end the war in Europe.

The United States was then able to focus more effectively on the war in the Pacific. The United States had been able to break the Japanese code; at the same time, Japan had been unable to crack US code thanks to the **Navajo Code Talkers**, who used the Navajo language, which Japan was unable to decipher. The US strategy of **island hopping** allowed it to take control of Japanese-held Pacific islands, proceeding closer to Japan itself despite **kamikaze** attacks on US ships, in which Japanese fighter pilots intentionally crashed their planes into these ships. President **Harry Truman** had taken power following FDR's death in 1945. Rather than force a US invasion of Japan, which would have resulted in huge numbers of casualties, he authorized the bombing of **Hiroshima** and **Nagasaki** in Japan, the only times that **nuclear weapons** have been used in conflict. The war ended with Japanese surrender on September 2, 1945.

Internment of Japanese Americans

In the United States, Japanese Americans were forced to live in internment camps. Under FDR's Executive Order 9066, these Americans were forced to give up their belongings and businesses and live in harsh military camps scattered throughout the West until the end of the war. They were surrounded by barbed wire and armed guards. Fred Korematsu argued that Executive Order 9066 was unconstitutional and fought to the Supreme Court for the rights of Japanese Americans, but the Court upheld FDR's order in *Korematsu v. United States*. Congress issued a formal apology to the survivors in 1988.

DID YOU KNOW?

Executive Order 9066 targeted Americans of Japanese descent, but other Americans suspected of having ties to the enemy due to their ethnicity, like German Americans, Italian Americans, and even some Aleutian Americans, were also forced into internment during WWII.

Postwar World

The **United Nations** was formed in the wake of the Second World War, modeled after the failed League of Nations. Unlike the League, however, it included a **Security Council** comprised of major world powers, with the power to militarily intervene for peacekeeping purposes in unstable global situations. With most of Europe destroyed, the victorious US and the Soviet Union emerged as the two global **superpowers**.

In 1945, Stalin, Churchill, and Roosevelt had met at the **Yalta Conference** to determine the future of Europe. The Allies had agreed on free elections for European countries following the fall of the fascist regimes. However, following the war, the USSR occupied Eastern Europe, preventing free elections. The United States saw this as a betrayal of the agreement at Yalta. Furthermore, while the US-led **Marshall Plan** began a program to rebuild Europe, the USSR consolidated its presence and power in eastern European countries, forcing them to reject aid from the Marshall Plan. This division would destroy the alliance between the Soviets and the West, leading to the **Cold War** between the two superpowers and the emergence of a **bipolar world**.

REVIEW QUESTIONS

11. What were the "Four Freedoms" about which Franklin D. Roosevelt spoke publicly to garner support for his position?

12. Why did the US first focus primarily on the European theater in its involvement in World War II?

13. Who helped the US develop a code that the Japanese were unable to decipher?

14. What empowers the United Nations to militarily intervene in unstable global situations?

15. What two global superpowers emerged after World War II?

Answer Key

1. The Panic of 1907 led to the establishment of the Federal Reserve.

2. Interventionism sought to spread US-style democracy, while isolationism focused on development at home.

3. Four events that led the US to enter World War I include: 1) German U-boats in the Atlantic; 2) the sinking of the *Lusitania*; 3) the Zimmerman Telegram; 4) growing nationalism.

4. The Emergency Quota Act (1921) and the National Origins Act (1924) were passed after World War I as a result of xenophobia and isolationism.

5. Marcus Garvey believed in self-sufficiency for African Americans, while the NAACP focused on integration.

6. Black Tuesday—the date of the 1929 stock market crash—is generally considered the start of the Great Depression.

7. The FDIC insures customer deposits against bank failure.

8. The Tennessee Valley Authority (TVA) was the first American public power company.

9. The PWA was established to develop infrastructure and provide construction jobs for the unemployed.

10. The Wagner Act ensured the right to unionize and established the National Labor Relations Board (NLRB).

11. FDR's Four Freedoms were: freedom of speech, freedom of religion, freedom from want, and freedom from fear.

12. The US believed that Hitler was the primary global threat.

13. The Navajo Code Talkers helped the US develop an unbreakable code.

14. The Security Council gives the United Nations the power to intervene using military force.

15. The United States and the Soviet Union emerged as the global superpowers after WWII.

9 Postwar and Contemporary United States

Cold War, Liberalism, and Social Change

Cold War at Home and Abroad

With the collapse of the relationship between the USSR and the US, distrust and fear of **communism** grew. Accusations of communist sympathies against public figures ran rampant during the **McCarthy Era** in the 1950s, reflecting domestic anxieties.

President Harry S Truman's **Truman Doctrine** stated that the US would support any country threatened by authoritarianism (communism), leading to the **Korean War** (1950 – 1953), a conflict between the US and Soviet-backed North Korean forces, which ended in a stalemate. The policy of **containment**, to contain Soviet (communist) expansion, defined US foreign policy; according to **domino theory**, once one country fell to communism, others would quickly follow. Other incidents included the **Bay of Pigs** invasion in Cuba (1961), a failed effort to topple the communist government of Fidel Castro, and the **Cuban Missile Crisis** (1962), when Soviet missiles were discovered in Cuba and a military crisis was narrowly averted, both under the administration of the popular President **John F. Kennedy**.

Meanwhile, in Southeast Asia, communist forces in North Vietnam were gaining power. Congress never formally declared war in Vietnam but gave the president authority to intervene militarily there through the **Gulf of Tonkin Resolution** (1964). However, this protracted conflict—the **Vietnam War**—also led to widespread domestic social unrest, which only increased with US deaths there, especially after the Vietnamese-led **Tet Offensive** (1968). The US ultimately withdrew from Vietnam. North Vietnamese forces, led by **Ho Chi Minh**, took over the entire country.

Liberalism and the War on Poverty

President Kennedy had envisioned a liberal United States in the tradition of the Progressives. His youth and charisma were inspiring to many Americans, and his assassination in 1963 was a shock. Kennedy's vice president Lyndon B. Johnson continued the liberal vision with the **Great Society**. LBJ embraced **liberalism**, believing that government should fight poverty at home, and play an interventionist role abroad (in this era, by fighting communism).

Johnson launched a **War on Poverty**, passing reform legislation to support the poor. The **Medicare Act** provided medical care to elderly Americans. The creation of the **Department of Housing and Urban Development** increased the federal role in housing and urban issues. Johnson's **Head Start** program provided early intervention for disadvantaged children before elementary school (and still does today). The **Elementary and Secondary Education Act** increased funding for primary and secondary education. Additionally, the **Immigration Act of 1965** overturned the provisions of the Emergency Quota Act, ending the racist limitations on immigrants to the US.

At the same time, LBJ's overseas agenda was increasingly unpopular. Adhering to containment and domino theory—US policy toward communism in an effort to stop its spread—Johnson drew the United States deeper into conflict in Southeast Asia. The **Vietnam War** was extremely unpopular in the US due to high casualties, the unpopular draft (which forced young American males to fight overseas), and what seemed to many to be the purposelessness of the war.

Student activists, organizing in the mold of the Civil Rights Movement, engaged in non-violent (and, at times, violent) protest against the Vietnam War. The rise of a **counterculture** among the youth—the development and popularity of **rock and roll music**, the culture of **hippies**, and changing concepts of drug use and sexuality—added to a sense of rebellion among Americans, usurping government authority and challenging traditional values.

REVIEW QUESTIONS

1. Which doctrine stated that the US would support any country threatened by authoritarianism (communism)?

2. What did the Gulf of Tonkin Resolution (1964) allow the president to do?

3. What were the two tenets of LBJ's liberalism?

4. Which of LBJ's programs provided early intervention for disadvantaged children before elementary school?

5. For what THREE reasons was the Vietnam War extremely unpopular in the US?

The Civil Rights Movement

The Civil Rights Movement

During the 1960s, the US experienced social and political change, starting with the election of the young and charismatic John F. Kennedy in 1960. Following JFK's assassination in 1963, President **Lyndon B. Johnson**'s administration saw the passage of liberal legislation in support of the poor and of civil rights. The **Civil Rights Movement**, led by activists like the **Rev. Dr. Martin Luther King, Jr.** and **Malcolm X**, fought for the rights of Black Americans, including the abolition of segregation, voting rights, and for better living standards for Black people throughout the country.

Figure 9.1. March on Washington

In 1954, the Supreme Court under Chief Justice Earl Warren found segregation unconstitutional in ***Brown v. Board of Education***, overturning its decision in *Plessy v. Ferguson*. *Brown* took place shortly after the desegregation of the armed forces. Public support for civil rights and racial equality was growing.

The **Southern Christian Leadership Conference (SCLC)** and Dr. King, a religious leader from Georgia, believed in civil disobedience, non-violent protest. In Montgomery, Alabama, **Rosa Parks**, a Black woman, was arrested for refusing to give up her seat to a white man on a bus. At the time, if a bus was crowded, Black people had to give up their seats to white passengers.

Leaders including Dr. King organized the **Montgomery Bus Boycott** to challenge segregation; the effort was ultimately successful. Building on their success, civil rights activists, now including many students and the **Student Nonviolent Coordinating Committee (SNCC)**, led peaceful protests and boycotts to protest segregation at lunch counters, in stores, at public pools, and other public places.

The movement grew to include voter registration campaigns organized by CORE, the Congress of Racial Equality, supported by students and other activists (both black and white) from around the country—the **Freedom Riders**, so-called because they rode buses from around the country to join the movement in the Deep South. SNCC and activists organized to protest segregation at government and public facilities and on university campuses. The movement continued to gain visibility as non-violent protesters were met with violence by the police and state authorities, including attacks by water cannons and police dogs in Alabama. Undaunted, activists continue to fight against segregation and unfair voting restrictions on Black Americans.

The Civil Rights Movement had national public attention, and had become a major domestic political issue. Civil rights workers organized the **March on Washington** in 1963, when Dr. King delivered his famous *I Have a Dream* speech. Widespread public support for civil rights legislation was impossible for the government to ignore. In 1964, Congress passed the **Civil Rights Act**, which outlawed segregation.

The Voting Rights Act

However, African Americans' voting rights were still not sufficiently protected. According to the Fifteenth and the Nineteenth Amendments, all African Americans—men and women—had the right to vote, but many Southern states had voting restrictions in place such as literacy tests and poll taxes, which disproportionately affected African Americans. Dr. King and civil rights workers organized a march from Selma to Montgomery, Alabama, to draw attention to this issue; however it ended in violence as marchers were attacked by police. In 1965, led by President Lyndon B. Johnson, Congress passed the **Voting Rights Act**, which forbade restrictions impeding the ability of African Americans to vote, including literacy tests. Separately, the **Twenty-Fourth Amendment** made poll taxes unconstitutional.

Black Empowerment

Meanwhile, **Malcolm X** was an outspoken proponent of **black empowerment**, particularly for African Americans in urban areas. Unlike Martin Luther King Jr., who believed in integration, Malcolm X and other activists, including groups like the **Black Panthers**, believed that African Americans should stay separate from whites to develop stronger communities.

Civil Rights for More Americans

The Civil Rights Movement extended beyond the Deep South. **Cesar Chavez** founded the **United Farm Workers (UFW)**, which organized Hispanic and migrant farm workers in California and the Southwest to advocate for unionizing and collective bargaining. Farm workers were underpaid and faced racial discrimination. The UFW used boycotts and non-violent tactics similar to those used by civil rights activists in the South; Cesar Chavez also used hunger strikes to raise awareness of the problems faced by farm workers.

The **American Indian Movement (AIM)** brought attention to injustices and discrimination suffered by Native Americans nationwide. Ultimately it was able to achieve more tribal autonomy and address problems facing Native American communities throughout the United States.

The Civil Rights Movement also included **feminist** activists who fought for fairer treatment of women in the workplace and for women's reproductive rights. The **National Organization for Women** and feminist leaders like **Gloria Steinem** led the movement for equal pay for women in the workplace. The landmark case of *Roe v. Wade* struck down federal restrictions on abortion.

In New York City in 1969, the **Stonewall riots** occurred in response to police repression of the gay community. These riots and subsequent organized activism are seen as the beginning of the LGBT rights movement. Harvey Milk, a city supervisor in San Francisco, was the first openly gay elected official in the United States. He was assassinated in 1978.

REVIEW QUESTIONS

6. Which case overturned the doctrine of separate but equal as established in *Plessy v. Ferguson*?

7. At which event did Dr. Martin Luther King, Jr. deliver his famous "I Have a Dream" speech?

8. What did the 1964 Civil Rights Act outlaw?

9. What did Malcolm X believe, in contrast to Martin Luther King?

10. Who did Cesar Chavez organize in California to advocate for unionizing and collective bargaining?

The Rise of Conservatism

Radical social change in the 1960s, coupled with the toll of the Vietnam War on the American public, many of whom had lost loved ones in the war, or served themselves in combat, led to backlash against liberalism. **Conservatism** strengthened in response to the heavy role of government in public life throughout the 1960s, high rates of government spending, and social challenges to traditional values. Due in great part to the escalation of the Vietnam War, LBJ announced his intention not to run for another term, and the conservative **Richard Nixon** became president in 1970.

Economic and International Crises

During the administration of the conservative President Richard Nixon, the conflict in Vietnam ended and a diplomatic relationship with China began. Nixon also oversaw economic reforms—he lifted the gold standard in an effort to stop **stagflation**, a phenomenon when both unemployment and inflation are high at the same time. Ending the gold standard reduced the value of the dollar in relation to other global currencies, and foreign investment in the United States increased. However, the Nixon administration was found to have engaged in corrupt practices. A burglary at the Democratic National Headquarters, based at the Watergate Hotel, was found to have been connected to the Oval Office. The **Watergate scandal** eventually forced Nixon to resign, and Vice President **Gerald Ford** took office for one term. Nixon's resignation further destroyed many Americans' faith in their government.

During the 1970s, the economy suffered due to US involvement in the Middle East. US support for Israel in the 1973 Yom Kippur War caused **OPEC** (the Organization of Petroleum Exporting Countries), led by Saudi Arabia and other allies of Arab foes of Israel, to boycott petroleum sales to the US using an economic embargo. As a result, oil prices skyrocketed. In the 1979 Iranian Revolution and the resulting **hostage crisis**, when the US Embassy in Tehran was taken over by anti-American activists, the economy suffered from another oil shock. While President Jimmy Carter had been able to negotiate peace between Israel and Egypt in the **Camp David Accords**, he was widely perceived as ineffective. Carter lost the presidency in 1980 to the conservative Republican **Ronald Reagan**.

Reagan championed domestic tax cuts and an aggressive foreign policy against the Soviet Union. The Reagan Revolution revamped the economic system, cutting taxes and government spending. According to supply-side economics (popularly known as *Reaganomics*), cutting taxes on the wealthy and providing investment incentives, wealth would "trickle down" to the middle and working classes and the poor. However, tax cuts forced Congress to cut or eliminate social programs that benefitted millions of those same Americans. Later, the **Tax Reform Act** of 1986 ended progressive income taxation.

Reagan and the Arms Race

Despite promises to lower government spending, the Reagan administration invested huge sums of money in the military. This investment in military technology—the **arms race** with the Soviet Union—helped bring about the end of the Cold War with the 1991 fall of the USSR and later, a new era of globalization. In addition to funding a general arms buildup and supporting measures to strengthen the military, the Reagan administration funded and developed advanced military technology to intimidate the Soviets, despite having signed the **Strategic Arms Limitation Treaties (SALT I and II)** limiting nuclear weapons and other strategic armaments in the 1970s. Ultimately, the US would outspend the USSR militarily, a precipitating factor to the fall of the Soviet Union.

Social Conservatism

The Reagan Revolution also ushered in an era of conservative values in the public sphere. After the Civil Rights Era, whose victories had occurred under the auspices of the Democratic Johnson administration, many Southern Democrats switched loyalties to the Republican Party. At the same time, the Democrats gained the support of African Americans and other groups who benefitted from civil rights and liberal legislation.

During the Reagan Era, conservative Republicans espoused a return to "traditional" values. **Christian fundamentalism** became popular, particularly among white conservatives. Groups like **Focus on the Family** lobbied against civil rights reform for women and advocated for traditional, two-parent, heterosexual families. Meanwhile, Reagan was criticized for failing to adequately respond to the crisis of the AIDS virus, which was sickening and killing thousands of Americans, especially Americans who were gay. Harsh prison sentences handed out as part of the "war on drugs" were criticized as racist, disproportionately harming Black and Hispanic Americans, as were conservative positions against social welfare programs.

REVIEW QUESTIONS

11. What economic situation results when both unemployment and inflation are high at the same time?

12. What caused OPEC's oil embargo?

13. What was the goal of supply-side economics (Reaganomics)?

14. With whom did the US wage and win an arms race under President Reagan?

_____

15. What group lobbied against civil rights reform for women and advocated for two-parent, heterosexual families?

_____

The End of the Cold War

The administration of **George H.W. Bush** signed the **Strategic Arms Reduction**, or **START, Treaty** with the Soviet Union in 1991, shortly before the dissolution of the USSR. Later, it would enter into force in 1994 between the US and the Russian Federation as an agreement to limit the large arsenals of strategic weapons possessed by both countries.

Unipolar World

With the collapse of the Soviet Union, the balance of international power changed. The bipolar world became a unipolar world, and the United States was the sole superpower. The first major crisis occurred in the Middle East when Iraq, led by **Saddam Hussein**, invaded oil-rich Kuwait. The US intervened—with the blessing of the United Nations, and the support of other countries. The resulting **Persian Gulf War**, or **Operation Desert Storm** (1991)—cemented its status as the world's sole superpower. Saddam's forces were driven from Kuwait, and Iraq was restrained by sanctions and no-fly zones.

With the election of President **Bill Clinton** in 1992, the US took an active role in international diplomacy, helping broker peace deals in the former Yugoslavia, Northern Ireland, and the Middle East. Clinton's election also indicated a more liberal era in American society. While conservative elements remained a strong force in politics and sectors of society, changing attitudes toward minorities in the public sphere and increased global communication (especially with the advent of the internet) were a hallmark of the 1990s.

Globalization and Social Liberalization

As part of **globalization**, the facilitation of global commerce and communication, the Clinton administration prioritized free trade. The United States signed the **North American Free Trade Agreement (NAFTA)** with Mexico and Canada, creating a free trade zone throughout North America, removing trade restrictions. The Clinton administration also eased financial restrictions in the United States, rolling back some of the limitations provided for under Glass-Steagal. These changes were controversial: many American jobs went overseas, especially manufacturing jobs, where labor was cheaper. Furthermore, globalization began facilitating the movement of people, particularly undocumented immigrants from Latin America seeking a better life in the United States. **Immigration reform** would be a major issue into the twenty-first century.

Clinton faced dissent in the mid-1990s with a conservative resurgence. A movement of young conservatives elected to Congress in 1994 promised a **Contract with America**, a conservative platform promising a return to lower taxes and traditional values. Clinton also came under fire for personal scandals: allegations of corrupt real estate investments in the Whitewater scandal and inappropriate personal behavior in the White House. These scandals fueled social conservatives and Christian fundamentalists who favored a return to the conservative era of the 1980s.

Despite these controversies and political division, society became increasingly liberal. Technology like the **internet** facilitated national and global communication, media, and business; minority groups like the LGBT community engaged in more advocacy; and environmental issues became more visible.

The Twenty-First Century

By the end of the twentieth century, the United States had established itself as the dominant global economic, military, and political power. Due to its role in global conflict from the Spanish-American War onwards, the US had established military bases and a military presence worldwide, in Europe, Asia, the Pacific, and the Middle East. The US dominated global trade: American corporations established themselves globally, taking advantage of free trade to exploit cheap labor pools and less restrictive manufacturing environments (at the expense of American workers). American culture was widely popular: since the early twentieth century, American pop culture like music, movies, television shows, and fashion has been enjoyed by millions of people around the world.

However, globalization also facilitated global conflict. While terrorism had been a feature of the twentieth century, the United States had been relatively untouched by large-scale terrorist attacks. That changed on **September 11, 2001**, when the terrorist group **al Qaeda** hijacked airplanes, attacking New York and Washington, D.C. in the largest attack on US soil since the Japanese bombing of Pearl Harbor. The 9/11 attacks triggered an aggressive military and foreign policy under the administration of President **George W. Bush**, who declared a *Global War on Terror*, an open-ended global conflict against terror organizations and their supporters.

Following the attacks, the US struck suspected al Qaeda bases in Afghanistan, beginning the **Afghanistan War**, during which time the US occupied the country. Suspected terrorist fighters captured there and elsewhere during the War on Terror were held in a prison in **Guantanamo Bay**, Cuba, which was controversial because it did not initially offer any protections afforded to prisoners of war under the Geneva Conventions.

President Bush believed in the doctrine of **preemption**, that if the US was aware of a threat, it should preemptively attack the source of that threat. Preemption would drive the invasion of Iraq in 2003. In 2003, the US attacked Iraq, believing that Iraq held **weapons of mass destruction** that could threaten the safety of the United States. This assumption was later revealed to be false; however, the United States promulgated the **Iraq War**, deposing Saddam

Hussein and supporting a series of governments until it withdrew its troops in 2011, leaving the country in a state of chaos.

At home, Congress passed the **USA Patriot Act** to respond to fears of more terrorist attacks on US soil; this legislation gave the federal government unprecedented—and, some argued, unconstitutional—powers of surveillance over the American public.

Despite the tense climate, social liberalization continued in the US. Following the Bush administration, during which tax cuts and heavy reliance on credit (especially in the housing market—the **Subprime Mortgage Crisis**) helped push the country into the **Great Recession**, the first African American president, **Barack Obama**, was elected in 2008. Under his presidency, the US emerged from the recession, ended major military operations in Iraq and Afghanistan, passed the Affordable Care Act, which reformed the health care system, and legalized same-sex marriage. The Obama administration also oversaw the passage of consumer protection acts, increased support for students, and safety nets for homeowners.

President Obama served two terms and was followed in 2016 by the election of President Donald Trump. During the later part of his presidency, the COVID-19 pandemic occured, leading to shutdowns and many people moving to remote work or losing their jobs. Despite this, the inflation rate in the U.S. hit a low in 2020; it then rose sharply in 2021. While serving as president, Donald Trump was impeached twice, once in 2019 and once in 2021, but was acquitted by the Senate in both cases. After the Trump administration, President Joe Biden was elected in 2020, and Kamala Harris became the first female Vice President. The Biden administration rejoined the World Health Organization and the Paris Climate Accord, and he served as president during the Russian invasion of Ukraine on February 24, 2022, and the Hamas attack on Israel on October 7, 2023. After the Biden administration, Donald Trump was reelected as president in 2024, becoming the second president to serve non-consecutive terms.

REVIEW QUESTIONS

16. Which event cemented the status of the United States as the world's sole superpower?

17. What did NAFTA create?

18. In what movement did young conservative members of Congress promise a return to lower taxes and traditional values?

19. When was the largest attack on US soil since the Japanese bombing of Pearl Harbor?

20. What gave the federal government powers of surveillance over the American public that some argued were unconstitutional?

_____

Answer Key

1. The Truman Doctrine stated that the US would support any country threatened by authoritarianism (communism).

2. The Gulf of Tonkin Resolution allowed the president to intervene militarily in Vietnam without a Congressional declaration of war.

3. The two tenets of LBJ's liberalism were fighting poverty at home and interventionism abroad.

4. Head Start began under LBJ to provide early intervention for disadvantaged children before elementary school.

5. The Vietnam War was extremely unpopular in the US because of the high number of casualties, the draft, and the lack of purpose.

6. *Brown v. Board of Education* (1954) overturned the doctrine of separate but equal as established in *Plessy v. Ferguson*.

7. Dr. Martin Luther King, Jr. delivered his famous "I Have a Dream" speech at the March on Washington in 1963.

8. The 1964 Civil Rights Act outlawed segregation.

9. Malcolm X believed that African Americans should stay separate from whites to develop stronger communities.

10. Cesar Chavez organized Hispanic and migrant farm workers in California to advocate for unionizing and collective bargaining.

11. Stagflation results when both unemployment and inflation are high at the same time.

12. OPEC launched an embargo against the United States in response to US support for Israel in the 1973 Yom Kippur War.

13. According to supply-side economics, wealth would "trickle down" to the middle and working classes and poor.

14. The US arms race was against the Soviet Union.

15. Focus on the Family was a major conservative group.

16. After the Gulf War (Operation Desert Storm), the United States was recognized for a time as the world's sole superpower.

17. NAFTA created a free trade zone throughout North America.

18. The Contract with America was a movement in which young conservative members of Congress promised a return to lower taxes and traditional values.

19. On September 11, 2001, terrorists attacked the United States in the largest attack on US soil since the bombing of Pearl Harbor.

20. The USA Patriot Act gave the federal government unprecedented and controversial powers of surveillance.

10 Geography and Civics Facts

United States Geography

The contiguous United States of America (USA) stretches across the North American continent from the Atlantic Ocean to the Pacific Ocean, from the Great Lakes to the Gulf of Mexico, from Puget Sound to the Rio Grande.

The major cities of the East Coast give way to the **Appalachian Mountains** in the east. The **Great Lakes** and the fertile valleys of the **Ohio, Mississippi, and Missouri Rivers** power the agricultural production of the Midwest and the Great Plains. Natural resources helped give rise to industrial centers in the rustbelt states. The **Mississippi Delta** and southern coastal plains are home to important agricultural products and are growing in population.

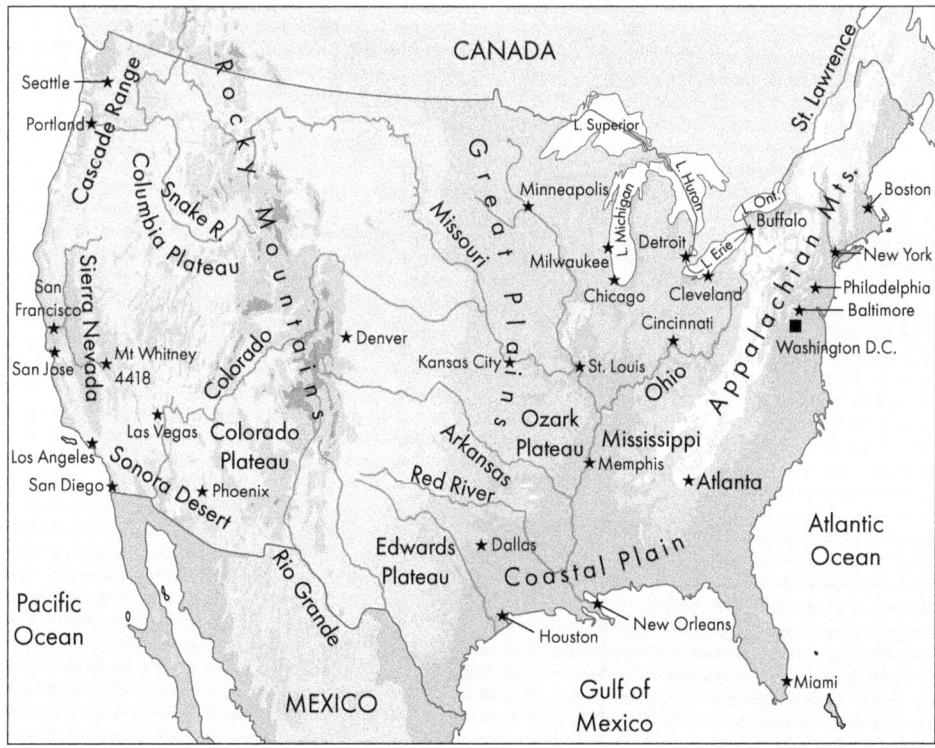

Figure 10.1. Major Landforms, Rivers, and Bodies of Water of the United States

HELPFUL HINT

The longest rivers in the United States are the Mississippi River and the Missouri River.

The **Rocky Mountains** and Southwestern deserts are home to some of the most extreme temperatures and beautiful landscapes of the world. They also contain valuable minerals and natural resources. The temperate rain forests of the Northwest and the Mediterranean climate of the California coast helped develop fertile farmland and support the growth of influential urban centers. The Pacific coast has vast fisheries and major harbors.

The USA's closest neighbors are **Canada** to the north and **Mexico** to the south. The US state of Alaska is separated from the other forty-eight states by the Canadian landmass, and only a few miles of water separate it from Russia. Another US state, Hawai'i, is completely surrounded by water in the warm southern Pacific Ocean.

Thirteen states border Canada: Maine, New Hampshire, Vermont, New York, Pennsylvania, Ohio, Michigan, Minnesota, North Dakota, Montana, Idaho, Washington, and Alaska. Pennsylvania and Ohio have maritime borders with Canada on Lake Erie, one of the Great Lakes. Four states border Mexico: Texas, New Mexico, Arizona, and California.

States and Territories

The United States has **fifty states** and several territories. The capital city of the United States is located in a federal district, not a state: the District of Columbia (DC). The capital is known as **Washington, DC**, and is governed by a municipal government. Each **state** has a certain level of independence and its own capital.

Figure 10.2. US States and Their Capitals

US territories are regions where the inhabitants are US citizens and pay taxes, but they do not have federal voting rights. Major US territories include Puerto Rico and the US Virgin Islands in the Caribbean; and Guam, American Samoa, and the Northern Mariana Islands in the Pacific Ocean.

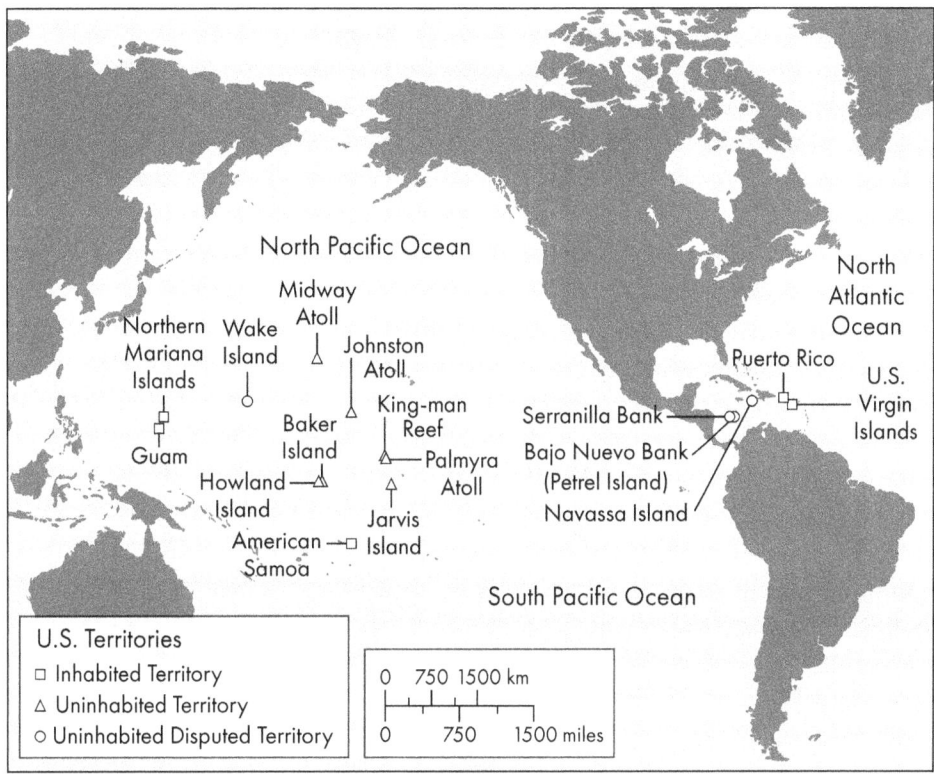

Figure 10.3. United States and US Territories

REVIEW QUESTIONS

1. The US has how many states?

2. Which states share borders with Canada?

3. Which states share borders with Mexico?

4. Is the capital city of the US located in a state?

5. Are people born in US territories considered US citizens?

CONTINUE

The United States Today

There are several important facts to know about the United States today in order to obtain your US citizenship.

Important People in the US Government

You should be familiar with certain leading political figures:

- President and Commander in Chief
- Vice President
- Speaker of the House
- Chief Justice of the Supreme Court

The answers to these questions change. To find the current answers, go here: uscis.gov/citizenship/testupdates

 DID YOU KNOW?
Elected in 2020, Kamala Harris is the first woman vice president in US history. Nancy Pelosi became the first woman to serve as Speaker of the House in 2006.

There are nine Supreme Court justices, 100 US senators, and 435 US representatives. These positions are covered in more detail in chapters 2 and 3.

Important US Landmarks

Landmarks are widely known markers. In the United States, there are several landmarks that are important symbols of American government and history.

The **Statue of Liberty** is located on Liberty Island, in New York Harbor, just off the coast of New York City. The statue's full name is "The Statue of Liberty Enlightening the World," and it is made of copper.

The statue was a gift from France to the United States, symbolizing friendship between the two nations. It was dedicated in 1886 and features a Roman goddess symbolizing liberty. She holds a document with July 4, 1776, inscribed in Roman numerals (the date of the Declaration of Independence) in one hand and a torch in the other.

Figure 10.4. Statue of Liberty

The **US Capitol** is the building where the House of Representatives and US Senate meet. The building opened in 1800 and is located on what is known as Capitol Hill, which is just to the east of the area in Washington, DC, known as the **National Mall**, an area with many government buildings, monuments, and public parks.

Figure 10.5. US Capitol

The National Mall is also closely bordered by the **White House**, the home of the US president, at its north end. Within the National Mall itself, and managed by the National Park Service, are the Washington Monument and the Lincoln Memorial.

Figure 10.6. The White House

The **Washington Monument** is a towering structure that honors the first president of the United States, George Washington. It stands 555 feet and 5 1/8 inches tall. It was the world's tallest building after it was completed in 1884, though it no longer holds this record. The tremendous scope of the monument was to honor Washington as a man of tremendous presence and importance as one of the nation's founding fathers.

Figure 10.7. Washington Monument and Lincoln Memorial at the National Mall

The **Lincoln Memorial** was made in the style of a Greek temple. It features a large statue of President Abraham Lincoln seated in a chair within it. It was completed in 1922 and also contains inscriptions of two of Lincoln's most famous speeches: The Gettysburg Address and the Second Inaugural Address. It honors Lincoln's achievements as president during the Civil War and his lasting legacy.

Independence Hall is the building in Philadelphia, Pennsylvania, in which the Declaration of Independence and the Constitution were adopted during the Second Continental Congress. The building was completed in 1753 and remains an important symbol of American democracy.

Figure 10.8. Independence Hall

Mount Rushmore is located in the small town of Keystone, South Dakota. It is a statue that features the faces of presidents George Washington, Thomas Jefferson, Abraham Lincoln, and Theodore Roosevelt carved directly into the rock of the Black Hills. The sculpture was created between 1927 and 1941 and was overseen by Gutzon Borglum and his son Lincoln Borglum. The sculpture honors these American presidents who are considered important to the development of the United States and its ideals.

Figure 10.9. Mount Rushmore Sculpture

Important Days and Holidays

There are three important days on which important events either take place or are commemorated. July 4, or **Independence Day** (also sometimes referred to as the Fourth of July), is an important national holiday. It commemorates the signing of the Declaration of Independence on July 4, 1776. The Declaration of Independence declared independence of the American colonies from Great Britain. (See chapter 6, "Revolution and the Early United States," for details.)

Each year, Americans are required to file their federal income tax returns with the Internal Revenue Service (IRS) on **April 15**, popularly called **Tax Day**. (Tax Day is not a holiday!)

Citizens are also encouraged to vote in federal elections, which always take place the Tuesday after the first Monday in November, which ranges from November 2 to November 8. This day is commonly known as **Election Day**. Legally, employers must give their employees time to go vote, but Election Day is not a holiday. Many localities, but not all, allow early voting in the days before Election Day, or offer extended voting hours on Election Day. To vote, one must be a US citizen, over eighteen, and registered to vote in the state in which they reside. Some states require voters to join a political party to vote in primaries. See the next section on Civics Facts for more information and details about voting.

 **DID YOU KNOW?**

The sculpture was constructed on land sacred to the Lakota Sioux people, who are indigenous to the Black Hills region. This mountain, the **Six Grandfathers** (sometimes called Cougar Mountain), was destroyed in the process of carving the sculpture.

The following are also **federal holidays**. This means that federal offices are closed on these days. Most of these are also recognized as state holidays, meaning state institutions (such as schools and state government) are also closed, but this is not always the case.

Memorial Day is a federal holiday that honors soldiers who died while serving in the military. Veterans Day is a federal holiday that honors people who are currently serving or have previously served in the military.

- New Year's Day (January 1)
- Martin Luther King Jr. Day (third Monday of January)
- Presidents' Day (third Monday in February)
- Memorial Day (last Monday of May)
- Labor Day (first Monday in September)
- Columbus Day (second Monday in October)
- Veterans Day (November 11)
- Thanksgiving (fourth Thursday of November)
- Christmas Day (December 25)

REVIEW QUESTIONS

6. In which building did the founding fathers adopt the US Constitution?

7. Which country gave the Statue of Liberty to the United States?

8. Which TWO American presidents are honored with memorials on the National Mall in Washington, DC?

9. In which building do the US Senate and House of Representatives meet?

10. List THREE national holidays of the United States.

Civics Facts

The Pledge of Allegiance

The **Pledge of Allegiance** originated in 1892 and has changed over time. The most recent and current version below was adopted in 1954 and includes the phrase "one nation under God." This phrase remains controversial because of the principles of separation of church and state as laid out in the US Constitution.

"I pledge allegiance to the Flag of the United States of America, and to the Republic for which it stands, one Nation under God, indivisible, with liberty and justice for all."

The pledge is typically said in front of an American flag with the right hand over the heart. The goal of the pledge is to show loyalty to the United States, a republic, NOT to the president or any specific person. People usually say the pledge as a group, often at the beginning of the school day, at government meetings, congressional sessions, and at US citizenship ceremonies.

The Flag

The American flag is an important symbol. Some legends say the first flag was sewn by a woman named Betsy Ross, who helped George Washington with the flag's design. Though there is little historical evidence of this, Ross remains an important symbol of American patriotism.

The first flag used to represent the United States in 1775 was called the Continental Colors, or the Grand Union Flag. It had some similarities to the British flag and was abandoned in 1777 for a flag with stars and stripes. This stars-and-stripes design went through many versions, though the thirteen alternating red and white stripes were constants except for one version that had

CONTINUE

fifteen. The number of stars has also varied, with the forty-eight-star flag seeing a long period of use from 1912 to 1959.

Today's American flag has thirteen stripes that symbolize the thirteen original colonies and fifty stars that symbolize the fifty American states.

0.10. American Flag Today

The Nation's First Motto

The current national motto, "In God We Trust" was made official in 1956, but there was an unofficial "first" national motto that was used earlier: E Pluribus Unum.

E Pluribus Unum means 'out of many, one' or 'we all become one'. It represents the joining of the 13 colonies to become one nation- America.

The National Anthem

The American national anthem is **"The Star-Spangled Banner."**

> O say can you see, by the dawn's early light,
>
> What so proudly we hailed at the twilight's last gleaming,
>
> Whose broad stripes and bright stars through the perilous fight,
>
> O'er the ramparts we watched, were so gallantly streaming?
>
> And the rocket's red glare, the bombs bursting in air,
>
> Gave proof through the night that our flag was still there;
>
> O say does that star-spangled banner yet wave
>
> O'er the land of the free and the home of the brave?

The anthem was composed by an American lawyer named **Francis Scott Key**, who had gone to negotiate for the release of a doctor friend of his who had been taken captive by the British during the **War of 1812**.

While Key was being guarded by the British on a ship in Chesapeake Bay, he could hear the Battle of Fort McHenry raging some 8 miles away. When he awoke the next morning—September 14, 1814—he expected to see the British flag flying over the fort, as it had seemed that the British would win the battle. When he saw the American flag instead, he was inspired to write a poem in four verses that was at first called "Defence of Fort M'Henry."

The poem caught on quickly but was not in widespread use at national events until President Woodrow Wilson ordered it be played at certain events in 1916. In 1931, the first verse of the poem, known as "The Star-Spangled Banner," became the official national anthem of the United States.

Becoming an American Citizen

People can become American citizens in a few different ways. The first and most common way is through birthright, or being born in America, under the conditions in the 14th amendment. Another way to become an American citizen is through deriving citizenship under the conditions that Congress sets, including the process of naturalization-- in which a foreigner is given the privileges of a native citizen. There are multiple categories of people who derive citizenship, including those who have lived in the United States for a certain amount of time (set by Congress) and are applying for naturalization, those who obtained citizenship after their parents naturalized in the United States, and those who are born to U.S. parents in another country (abroad).

Rights and Responsibilities of American Citizens

American citizens have a responsibility to **vote**. All American citizens over eighteen are eligible to vote, with a few exceptions (such as being convicted of certain crimes or being declared mentally incapacitated).

To vote, citizens must register as a voter in their state. Voting laws differ in each state, as does the manner in which elections are held (e.g., early voting, mail-in voting). In some states, people must declare an affiliation with a political party to vote in primary elections. In other states, people may vote in a primary election without making a party affiliation choice.

There are many different elections held at various times. National or federal elections are for federal offices like president, senator, and US representative. State elections are for state offices like governor and state senator or representative. Local elections are for offices like mayor, school board, and city council.

It is each citizen's responsibility to find out when elections are held, who is running, and where to go to vote. Voting information is often found on each state's voter information webpage. Voting is a very important part of American democracy and is a way for individual citizens to make their opinions known to those in government.

Another responsibility of citizenship is serving on a **jury**. A jury is a group of people who hear evidence in a court and decide whether a person is guilty or not guilty of having committed a crime. All citizens over eighteen are eligible to serve on juries (though there are some exceptions, similar to voting eligibility).

Citizens are most often notified of jury duty by mail. Failure to appear for jury duty is a crime. Because jury duty is so important, federal law prohibits employers from terminating people who need time off to serve on a jury. That is, if you are called to jury duty, your employer must let you miss work to attend.

All males from eighteen to twenty-five residing in the United States are also required by law to register for selective service. It does not matter if they are citizens or not. This is to ensure that a draft would be fair, if one is needed. It is also considered one's civic duty to America.

Registering for the selective service does not mean the person will be called into active military duty. The selective service would only draft young men into the armed forces in a wartime crisis situation. The last time this occurred was in 1973.

Outside of these responsibilities, American citizens can and should engage with their government in other ways. They can call, write, or email their senator or congressperson. They can volunteer to work on a political campaign or even run for office themselves. They can attend local civic meetings, school board meetings, or city council meetings. They can express their political opinions by writing to a newspaper. The possibilities are many, but the more each citizen is involved, the stronger American democracy is.

Paying Taxes

One key responsibility and civic duty of every American citizen is to pay federal taxes. It's important to pay federal taxes because the money is used to fund the federal government. It is also required by law under the 16th Amendment of the U.S. Constitution.

American Innovations

America has been at the forefront of many scientific and technological advances, including the creation of the automobile, skyscrapers, the airplane, the assembly line, the integrated circuit, as well as one of the most famous-- the light bulb (which was invented by Thomas Edison).

REVIEW QUESTIONS

11. Which phrase was added to the Pledge of Allegiance in 1954?

12. During what war was the "Star-Spangled Banner" written?

13. How old must a citizen be to vote?

14. What does a jury do?

15. Between what ages must all men living in the United States register for the selective service?

Answer Key

1. There are fifty states in the USA.

2. Alaska, Washington, Idaho, Montana, North Dakota, Minnesota, Michigan, Ohio, Pennsylvania, New York, Vermont, New Hampshire, and Maine share borders with Canada.

3. California, Arizona, New Mexico, and Texas share borders with Mexico.

4. No, it is in a federal district, the District of Columbia.

5. Yes, people born in US territories are US citizens.

6. Independence Hall is where the US Constitution was adopted.

7. France gave the Statue of Liberty to the United States.

8. George Washington and Abraham Lincoln have memorials on the National Mall.

9. The US Senate and House of Representatives meet in the US Capitol building.

10. Any three of the following: New Year's Day, Martin Luther King Jr. Day, Presidents' Day, Independence Day, Memorial Day, Labor Day, Columbus Day, Veterans Day, Thanksgiving, Christmas

11. The phrase "one nation under God" was added to the Pledge of Allegiance in 1954.

12. The "Star-Spangled Banner" was written during the War of 1812.

13. A citizen must be eighteen years old to vote.

14. A jury decides if a person is guilty or not guilty of a crime.

15. All men living in the US between the ages of eighteen and twenty-five must register for the selective service.

11 USCIS Civics Test

As of October 20, 2025, USCIS is administering the 2025 civics test to N-400 applicants.

The questions and answer explanations below are provided by USCIS; see **https://www.uscis.gov/sites/default/files/document/questions-and-answers/2025-Civics-Test-128-Questions-and-Answers.pdf**. Some questions will have multiple correct answer choice options which are separated by a semicolon (;). Any of those listed would be considered correct.

A USCIS officer will ask you these questions in person. Your officer will choose twenty questions from the bank of 128. To pass the test, you must answer 12 of the 20 questions correctly.

If you are sixty-five years or older and have been living in the United States as a lawful permanent resident for twenty years or more, you only need to study the questions marked with an asterisk. The exam is an oral exam. You will be asked 10 of the following questions. You must answer 6 correctly in order to pass.

1. What is the form of government of the United States?

2. What is the supreme law of the land? *

3. Name one thing the U.S. Constitution does.

4. The U.S. Constitution starts with the words "We the People." What does "We the People" mean?

5. How are changes made to the U.S. Constitution?

6. What does the Bill of Rights protect?

7. How many amendments does the U.S. Constitution have? *

8. Why is the Declaration of Independence important?

9. What founding document said the American colonies were free from Britain?

10. Name two important ideas from the Declaration of Independence and the U.S. Constitution.

11. The words "Life, Liberty, and the pursuit of Happiness" are in what founding document?

12. What is the economic system of the United States? *

13. What is the rule of law?

14. Many documents influenced the U.S. Constitution. Name one.

15. There are three branches of government. Why?

16. Name the three branches of government.

17. The President of the United States is in charge of which branch of government?

18. What part of the federal government writes laws?

19. What are the two parts of the U.S. Congress?

20. Name one power of the U.S. Congress. *

21. How many U.S. senators are there?

22. How long is a term for a U.S. senator?

23. Who is one of your state's U.S. senators now?

24. How many voting members are in the House of Representatives?

25. How long is a term for a member of the House of Representatives?

26. Why do U.S. representatives serve shorter terms than U.S. senators?

27. How many senators does each state have?

28. Why does each state have two senators?

29. Name your U.S. representative.

30. What is the name of the Speaker of the House of Representatives now? *

31. Who does a U.S. senator represent?

32. Who elects U.S. senators?

33. Who does a member of the House of Representatives represent?

34. Who elects members of the House of Representatives?

35. Some states have more representatives than other states. Why?

36. The President of the United States is elected for how many years? *

37. The President of the United States can serve only two terms. Why?

38. What is the name of the President of the United States now? *

39. What is the name of the Vice President of the United States now? *

40. If the president can no longer serve, who becomes president?

41. Name one power of the president.

42. Who is Commander in Chief of the U.S. military?

43. Who signs bills to become laws?

44. Who vetoes bills? *

45. Who appoints federal judges?

46. The executive branch has many parts. Name one.

47. What does the President's Cabinet do?

48. What are two Cabinet-level positions?

49. Why is the Electoral College important?

50. What is one part of the judicial branch?

51. What does the judicial branch do?

52. What is the highest court in the United States? *

53. How many seats are on the Supreme Court?

54. How many Supreme Court justices are usually needed to decide a case?

55. How long do Supreme Court justices serve?

56. Supreme Court justices serve for life. Why?

57. Who is the Chief Justice of the United States now?

58. Name one power that is only for the federal government.

59. Name one power that is only for the states.

60. What is the purpose of the 10th Amendment?

61. Who is the governor of your state now? *

62. What is the capital of your state?

63. There are four amendments to the U.S. Constitution about who can vote. Describe one of them.

64. Who can vote in federal elections, run for federal office, and serve on a jury in the United States?

65. What are three rights of everyone living in the United States?

66. What do we show loyalty to when we say the Pledge of Allegiance? *

67. Name two promises that new citizens make in the Oath of Allegiance.

68. How can people become United States citizens?

69. What are two examples of civic participation in the United States?

70. What is one way Americans can serve their country?

71. Why is it important to pay federal taxes?

72. It is important for all men age 18 through 25 to register for the Selective Service. Name one reason why.

73. The colonists came to America for many reasons. Name one.

74. Who lived in America before the Europeans arrived? *

75. What group of people was taken and sold as slaves?

76. What war did the Americans fight to win independence from Britain?

77. Name one reason why the Americans declared independence from Britain.

78. Who wrote the Declaration of Independence? *

79. When was the Declaration of Independence adopted?

80. The American Revolution had many important events. Name one.

81. There were 13 original states. Name five.

82. What founding document was written in 1787?

83. The Federalist Papers supported the passage of the U.S. Constitution. Name one of the writers.

84. Why were the Federalist Papers important?

85. Benjamin Franklin is famous for many things. Name one.

86. George Washington is famous for many things. Name one. *

87. Thomas Jefferson is famous for many things. Name one.

88. James Madison is famous for many things. Name one.

89. Alexander Hamilton is famous for many things. Name one.

90. What territory did the United States buy from France in 1803?

91. Name one war fought by the United States in the 1800s.

92. Name the U.S. war between the North and the South.

93. The Civil War had many important events. Name one.

94. Abraham Lincoln is famous for many things. Name one. *

95. What did the Emancipation Proclamation do?

96. What U.S. war ended slavery?

97. What amendment says all persons born or naturalized in the United States, and subject to the jurisdiction thereof, are U.S. citizens?

98. When did all men get the right to vote?

99. Name one leader of the women's rights movement in the 1800s.

100. Name one war fought by the United States in the 1900s.

101. Why did the United States enter World War I?

102. When did all women get the right to vote?

103. What was the Great Depression?

104. When did the Great Depression start?

105. Who was president during the Great Depression and World War II?

106. Why did the United States enter World War II?

107. Dwight Eisenhower is famous for many things. Name one.

108. Who was the United States' main rival during the Cold War?

109. During the Cold War, what was one main concern of the United States?

110. Why did the United States enter the Korean War?

111. Why did the United States enter the Vietnam War?

112. What did the civil rights movement do?

113. Martin Luther King, Jr. is famous for many things. Name one. *

114. Why did the United States enter the Persian Gulf War?

115. What major event happened on September 11, 2001 in the United States? *

116. Name one U.S. military conflict after the September 11, 2001 attacks.

117. Name one American Indian tribe in the United States.

118. Name one example of an American innovation.

119. What is the capital of the United States?

120. Where is the Statue of Liberty?

121. Why does the flag have 13 stripes? *

122. Why does the flag have 50 stars?

123. What is the name of the national anthem?

124. The Nation's first motto was "E Pluribus Unum." What does that mean?

125. What is Independence Day?

126. Name three national U.S. holidays. *

127. What is Memorial Day?

128. What is Veterans Day?

Answer Key

1. A republic; constitution-based federal republic; representative democracy

2. The Constitution

3. Forms the government; defines powers of the government; defines the parts of government; protects the rights of the people

4. Self-government; popular sovereignty; consent of the governed; that people should govern themselves; it is (an example of) a social contract

5. Amendments; the amendment process

6. The basic rights of Americans; the basic rights of people living in the United States

7. Twenty-seven (27)

8. It says America is free from British control; it says all people are created equal; it identifies inherent rights; it identifies individual freedoms.

9. Declaration of Independence

10. Equality; liberty; social contract; natural rights; limited government; self-government

11. Declaration of Independence

12. Capitalism; free market economy

13. Everyone must follow the law; leaders must obey the law; government must obey the law; no one is above the law

14. Declaration of Independence; Articles of Confederation; Federalist Papers; Anti-Federalist Papers; Virginia Declaration of Rights; Fundamental Orders of Connecticut; Mayflower Compact; Iroquois Great Law of Peace

15. So one part does not become too powerful; checks and balances; separation of powers

16. Legislative, executive, and judicial; Congress, the president, and the courts

17. Executive branch

18. (U.S.) Congress; (U.S. or national) legislature; legislative branch

19. Senate and House (of Representatives)

20. Writes laws; declares war; makes the federal budget

21. One hundred (100)

22. Six (6) years

23. Answers will vary by state, you can find your state's senators at: https://www.congress.gov/members. District of Columbia residents and residents of U.S. territories should answer that D.C. (or the territory) has no U.S. senators.

24. Four hundred thirty-five (435)

25. Two (2) years

26. To more closely follow public opinion

27. Two (2)

28. Equal representation (for small states); The Great Compromise (Connecticut Compromise)

29. Answers will vary, you can find your U.S. representatives at: https://www.congress.gov/members. Residents of territories with nonvoting Delegates or Resident Commissioners may provide the name of that Delegate or Commissioner. Also acceptable is any statement that the territory has no (voting) representatives in Congress.

30. This answer can change. Visit https://www.uscis.gov/citizenship/find-study-materials-and-resources/check-for-test-updates for the name of the Speaker of the House of Representatives.

31. Citizens of their state; people of their state

32. Citizens from their state

33. Citizens in their (congressional) district; citizens in their district; people from their (congressional) district; people in their district

34. Citizens from their (congressional) district

35. (Because of) the state's population; (because) they have more people; (because) some states have more people

36. Four (4) years

37. (Because of) the 22nd Amendment; to keep the president from becoming too powerful

38. This answer can change. Visit https://www.uscis.gov/citizenship/find-study-materials-and-resources/check-for-test-updates for the name of the President of the United States.

39. Visit https://www.uscis.gov/citizenship/find-study-materials-and-resources/check-for-test-updates for the name of the Vice President of the United States.

40. The Vice President (of the United States)

41. Signs bills into law; vetoes bills; enforces laws; Commander in Chief (of the military); chief diplomat; appoints federal judges

42. The President (of the United States)

43. The President (of the United States)

44. The President (of the United States)

45. The President (of the United States)

46. President (of the United States); Cabinet; Federal departments and agencies

47. Advises the President (of the United States)

48. Attorney General; Secretary of Agriculture; Secretary of Commerce; Secretary of Education; Secretary of Energy; Secretary of Health and Human Services; Secretary of Homeland Security; Secretary of Housing and Urban Development; Secretary of the Interior; Secretary of Labor; Secretary of State; Secretary of Transportation; Secretary of the Treasury; Secretary of Veterans Affairs; Secretary of War (Defense); Vice-President; Administrator of the Environmental Protection Agency; Administrator of the Small Business Administration; Director of the Central Intelligence Agency; Director of the Office of Management and Budget; Director of National Intelligence; United States Trade Representative

49. It decides who is elected president; it provides a compromise between the popular election of the president and congressional selection.

50. Supreme Court; Federal Courts

51. Reviews laws; explains laws; resolves disputes (disagreements) about the law; decides if a law goes against the (U.S.) Constitution

52. Supreme Court

53. Nine (9)

54. Five (5)

55. (For) life; lifetime appointment; (until) retirement

56. To be independent (of politics); to limit outside (political) influence

57. This answer can change. Visit https://www.uscis.gov/citizenship/find-study-materials-and-

resources/check-for-test-updates for the name of the Chief Justice of the United States.

58. Print paper money; mint coins; declare war; create an army; make treaties; set foreign policy

59. Provide schooling and education; provide protection (police); provide safety (fire departments); give a driver's license; approve zoning and land use

60. (It states that the) powers not given to the federal government belong to the states or to the people.

61. This answer will change. Answers will vary by state and can be found at https://www.uscis.gov/citizenship/find-study-materials-and-resources/check-for-test-updates. District of Columbia residents should answer that D.C. does not have a governor.

62. Answers will vary. District of Columbia residents should answer that D.C. is not a state and does not have a capital. Residents of U.S. territories should name the capital of the territory.

63. Citizens eighteen (18) and older (can vote); you don't have to pay (a poll tax) to vote; any citizen can vote/women and men can vote; a male citizen of any race (can vote).

64. Citizens; citizens of the United States; U.S. citizens

65. Freedom of expression; freedom of speech; freedom of assembly; freedom to petition the government; freedom of religion; the right to bear arms

66. The United States; the flag

67. Give up loyalty to other countries; defend the (U.S.) Constitution; obey the laws of the United States; serve in the military (if needed); serve (help, do important work for) the nation (if needed); be loyal to the United States

68. Be born in the United States, under the conditions set by the 14th Amendment; naturalize; derive citizenship (under conditions set by Congress)

69. Vote; run for office; join a political party; help with a campaign; join a civic group; join a community group; give an elected official your opinion (on an issue); contact elected officials; support or oppose an issue or policy; write to a newspaper

70. Vote; pay taxes; obey the law; serve in the military; run for office; work for local, state, or federal government

71. Required by law; all people pay to fund the federal government; required by the (U.S.) Constitution (16th Amendment); civic duty

72. Required by law; civic duty; makes the draft fair, if needed

73. Freedom; political liberty; religious freedom; economic opportunity; escape persecution

74. American Indians; Native Americans

75. Africans; people from Africa

76. American Revolution; the (American) Revolutionary War; War for (American) Independence

77. High taxes; taxation without representation; British soldiers stayed in Americans' houses (boarding, quartering); they did not have self-government; Boston Massacre; Boston Tea Party (Tea Act); Stamp Act; Sugar Act; Townshend Acts; Intolerable (Coercive) Acts

78. (Thomas) Jefferson

79. July 4, 1776

80. (Battle of) Bunker Hill; Declaration of Independence; Washington Crossing the Delaware (Battle of Trenton); (Battle of) Saratoga; Valley Forge (Encampment); (Battle of) Yorktown (British surrender at Yorktown)

81. New Hampshire; Massachusetts; Rhode Island; Connecticut; New York; New Jersey; Pennsylvania; Delaware; Maryland; Virginia; North Carolina; South Carolina; Georgia

82. (U.S.) Constitution

83. (James) Madison; (Alexander) Hamilton; (John) Jay; Publius

84. They helped people understand the (U.S.) Constitution; they supported passing the (U.S.) Constitution.

85. Founded the first free public libraries; First Postmaster General of the United States; helped write the Declaration of Independence; inventor; U.S. diplomat

86. "Father of Our Country"; First president of the United States; General of the Continental Army; President of the Constitutional Convention

87. Writer of the Declaration of Independence; Third president of the United States; Doubled the size of the United States (Louisiana Purchase); First Secretary of State; founded the University of Virginia; writer of the Virginia Statute on Religious Freedom

88. "Father of the Constitution"; Fourth president of the United States; President during the War of 1812; one of the writers of the Federalist Papers

89. First Secretary of the Treasury; one of the writers of the Federalist Papers; helped establish the First Bank of the United States; aide to General George Washington; member of the Continental Congress

90. Louisiana Territory; Louisiana

91. War of 1812; Mexican-American War; Civil War; Spanish-American War

92. The Civil War

93. (Battle of) Fort Sumter; Emancipation Proclamation; (Battle of) Vicksburg; (Battle of) Gettysburg; Sherman's March; (Surrender at) Appomattox; (Battle of) Antietam/Sharpsburg; Lincoln was assassinated

94. Freed the slaves (Emancipation Proclamation); saved (or preserved) the Union; led the United States during the Civil War; 16th president of the United States; delivered the Gettysburg Address

95. Freed the slaves; freed slaves in the Confederacy; freed slaves in the Confederate states; freed slaves in most Southern states

96. The Civil War

97. 14th Amendment

98. After the Civil War; during Reconstruction; (with the) 15th Amendment; 1870

99. Susan B. Anthony; Elizabeth Cady Stanton; Sojourner Truth; Harriet Tubman; Lucretia Mott; Lucy Stone

100. World War I; World War II; Korean War; Vietnam War; (Persian) Gulf War

101. Because Germany attacked U.S. (civilian) ships; to support the Allied Powers (England, France, Italy, and Russia); to oppose the Central Powers (Germany, Austria-Hungary, the Ottoman Empire, and Bulgaria)

102. 1920; after World War I; (with the) 19th Amendment

103. Longest economic recession in modern history

104. The Great Crash (1929); stock market crash of 1929

105. (Franklin) Roosevelt

106. (Bombing of) Pearl Harbor; Japanese attacked Pearl Harbor; to support the Allied Powers (England, France, and Russia); to oppose the Axis Powers (Germany, Italy, and Japan)

107. General during World War II; President at the end of (during) the Korean War; 34th president of the United States; Signed the Federal-Aid Highway Act of 1956 (Created the Interstate System)

108. Soviet Union; USSR; Russia

109. Communism; nuclear war

110. To stop the spread of communism

111. To stop the spread of communism

112. Fought to end racial discrimination

113. Fought for civil rights; worked for equality for all Americans; worked to ensure that people would "not be judged by the color of their skin, but by the content of their character"

114. To force the Iraqi military from Kuwait

115. Terrorists attacked the United States; terrorists took over two planes and crashed them into the World Trade Center in New York City; terrorists took over a plane and crashed into the Pentagon in Arlington, Virginia; terrorists took over a plane originally aimed at Washington, D.C., and crashed in a field in Pennsylvania

116. (Global) War on Terror; War in Afghanistan; War in Iraq

117. Apache; Blackfeet; Cayuga; Cherokee; Cheyenne; Chippewa; Choctaw; Creek; Crow; Hopi; Huron; Inupiat; Lakota; Mohawk; Mohegan; Navajo; Oneida; Onondaga; Pueblo; Seminole; Seneca; Shawnee; Sioux; Teton; Tuscarora. For a complete list of tribes, please visit bia.gov/service/tribal-leaders-directory.

118. Light bulb; automobile (cars, internal combustion engine); skyscrapers; airplane; assembly line; landing on the moon; integrated circuit (IC)

119. Washington, D.C.

120. New York (Harbor); Liberty Island. Also acceptable are New Jersey, near New York City, and on the Hudson (River).

121. (Because there were) 13 original colonies; (because the stripes) represent the original colonies

122. (Because there is) one star for each state; (because) each star represents a state; (because there are) 50 states

123. The Star-Spangled Banner

124. Out of many, one; we all become one

125. A holiday to celebrate U.S. independence (from Britain); the country's birthday

126. New Year's Day; Martin Luther King, Jr. Day; Presidents Day (Washington's Birthday); Memorial Day; Juneteenth; Independence Day; Labor Day; Columbus Day; Veterans Day; Thanksgiving Day; Christmas Day

127. A holiday to honor soldiers who died in military service

128. A holiday to honor people in the (U.S.) military; a holiday to honor people who have served (in the U.S. military)

www.ingramcontent.com/pod-product-compliance
Lightning Source LLC
Chambersburg PA
CBHW081236170426
43198CB00017B/2772